GODDESS

When She Rules

GODDESS
When She Rules

EXPRESSIONS BY
CONTEMPORARY WOMEN

EDITED BY
CATHERINE L. SCHWEIG

WITH

TAMMY STONE TAKAHASHI

JULIA W. PRENTICE

SANDRA M. ALLAGAPEN

GOLDEN DRAGONFLY PRESS
Amherst, Massachusetts
2018

SECOND PRINT EDITION, January 2018
SECOND EBOOK EDITION, January 2018

FIRST PRINT EDITION, December 2017
FIRST EBOOK EDITION, December 2017

Front cover art *LA MEDECINE DE LA TORTUE*
© 2018 Caroline Manière

Illustrations by
Shailie Dubois (pages 216, 237)
and Jill Cooper (pages xxvi, 66, 138).

First published in the United States of America
by Golden Dragonfly Press, 2017.

www.goldendragonflypress.com

To the Goddess in all her forms,
and those who wave her flag with us
as she comes into her reign.

To the ruling Goddess of my heart
Srimati Radharani, Krishna's beloved Swamini.

Contents

The Eternal Goddess 1

The Mythical Goddess 67

The Goddess Within 139

Acknowledgements

The genesis of this book was in the spirit of the Journey of the Heart women's spiritual poetry community. The participants united in a sisterhood that spontaneously reverberated with Goddess energy! It was only a matter of time therefore, before the request for a Goddess anthology fell upon the sisterhood's fertile soil. And so it was, five years after I founded the project online that this anthology emerged.

From a seed that took root in December 2016, the offerings to our Goddess book first began pouring in on March 1st to the happy tunes of spring birdcalls. Through summer it flowered wildly inundating us with essays and poems that wiggled and kicked. By autumn gestation was nearly complete. When the project came full circle, in December of 2017—as winter solstice neared and longings for hibernating-by-fireplaces-with-good-books peaked— this anthology was birthed, with a singular, mighty cry declaring: "I am alive!" Yes, it's a girl! And she's here to show us the Goddess.

Much gratitude, therefore, to all the women who entrusted us with their Goddess visions, their reflections, their insights, and their dreams. To the wise words that trickled out of you in the middle of the night, the poems you barely caught while stepping out of the shower, the essays you carefully unearthed from your core. Thank you for giving us your feral souls, your naked hearts and those juicy realizations you'd been brewing for decades, perhaps even lifetimes. Together, we've woven an alluringly eclectic portrait of the Goddess with our collected voice: yet another colorful patch in the quilt of a new Goddess paradigm.

My heartfelt appreciations to my very dedicated and talented team of "Poetry Midwives" who delivered our Divine Feminine triplets: Julia W. Prentice for "The Eternal Goddess," Sandra M. Allagapen for "The Mythical Goddess" and Tammy Stone Takahashi for "The Goddess Within." Thank you for the endless tasks that went into organizing, choosing, sorting, editing and formatting the writings of our 93 contributors. Thank you also to Kim Buskala for her overall support and additional editorial participation. The four of you made our moonlit dances around the bonfire of these illuminating voices wildly inspiring to me.

I offer my respectful *pranams* and gratitude to renowned author, spiritual teacher, and practicing Yogini of nearly 50 years, Sally Kempton for having generously written our Foreword. It is an honor to have you welcome readers into our anthology.

Thank you to the inspired and gifted artists who gave us beautiful visual glimpses into some of the endless faces of the Goddess: Jill Cooper and Shailie Dubois for the book's interior drawings, and Caroline Manière for our gorgeous cover art.

I'll always be in debt to and in awe of our publisher, Alice, of Golden Dragonfly Press—ever a good and wickedly skilled witch in my eyes—who works her magnificent magic on our manuscripts every time. I can't thank you enough, Alice!

Lastly, I'd like to acknowledge a few of the many ways that the Goddess has appeared over the course of my own life: as Mother Nature for the myriad ways she comforts and enchants. As the fairies that my mother first introduced me to in picture books, and as the sweet lullabies she sang. As the primal, exhilarating force in naturally birthing both my own two children, the ten years of breastfeeding that followed, the fierce love of Motherhood. As Yemanja the ocean Goddess in a beautiful blue gown, who father brought back from Brazil one year. As the Aztec and Catholic Goddesses of my childhood: Tonantzin and the Virgin of Guadalupe, on whose festival day this book was released. As Sita, Laxmi, Sarasvati, Durga, and Kali, who danced into my life during my 20's in each of their own special ways. As Tulasi Devi—Queen of Vrindavan—the plant Goddess who graced my home for years. As the river Goddesses, Ganga and Yamuna—whom the daughter I lost in my womb was named after. As Yoga Maya (Paurnamasi) who was so adored by my Guru, he wrote me long letters of her glories from his seaside ashram in India. And *especially,* as Radha—my spiritual namesake—the Supreme Divine Feminine in the Bhagavat Purana, whose unlimited divine Shaktis (feminine energies) flow through all life.

From the bottom of my heart, I thank my spouse and partner-in-life, Graham, whose work revolves around bringing out the

Goddess in ancient Sanskrit texts, and whose encouragement of my *seva* (service) unto that same Goddess is never-ending.

Most of all, in the context of this work, I offer my deepest gratitude to She who made the contributors to this volume her musical instruments and played us in harmonious unison. To the Sacred Feminine conducting our symphony, the Goddess who turned our voices into song. May our songs travel across the meadows and seas, through prejudices and walls, over mountains and politics, into all the little nooks and crannies of those who need to hear them the most!

"The Goddess has never been lost.
It is just that some of us have forgotten how to find her."

Patricia Monaghan

Foreword

This world is the body of the Goddess. That's what the old Goddess traditions tell us. The Goddess, they say, is Life itself. Because we live within her—and because she is actually living *us*—we are often blind to her presence. A well-nourished infant takes the mother's love and protection for granted. In the same way, we who live embedded in this world don't see the sacred Presence that is powering our very existence.

Human beings are waking up to sacred Presence in the physical world. And this, in time, leads more and more of us to consider the possibility that divine Presence might actually turn out to be feminine. Not necessarily feminine in the sense of gender, but feminine in an energetic sense. That's what this book is all about.

Goddess: When She Rules expresses an emerging modern revelation about the sacred feminine. Many of us today experience what can only be called Goddess epiphanies—palpable experiences of sacred female Presence. The women who contributed to this book have experienced these epiphanies, in unique, personal and wildly specific ways. In these pages, they celebrate their realizations through poetry, confessional prose, and insightful observation. To read their words is to realize how radically our view of the sacred feminine—and therefore of religion—is being transformed.

Historically, western popular religion has either ignored the sacred feminine or equated her mostly with the physical world and the grossness of matter. She is 'Mother Nature.' She is Gaia. In her personal forms, she often appears as goddess-figures who mirror the masculine experience of the feminine—the virgin, the mother/ caretaker, the crone, the whore, or the disembodied muse. This version of Goddess worship associates her with archaic forms of nature religion, magic, animism, and shamanism. To love Goddess as nature can be exquisite—but it is also limiting. We may deeply love the Earth, honor her as the Mother, and strive to protect her. But when we think of Goddess as personified Nature, it is also not so difficult to objectify her as the field to be plowed, the erupting volcano, the abundant ocean or the minerals beneath the earth.

In fact, the traditional view of the sacred feminine usually casts her as the generative, nurturing field for human (often, masculine) creativity, always available to provide a womb for human projects, always offering her substance and wealth for human use. She's ambiguous, of course: although ready to nourish and protect, she is also dangerously prone to upheavals, storms, and other weather events. As nature, she is the terrible mother as well as the nurturing mother. Therefore, she must be controlled.

In old patriarchal cultures, this attitude can extend through every domain of life. Woman is seen as the womb within which the masculine casts his seed, as the earth is simply the field within which the farmer sows crops. She needs to be dominated, flattered (when necessary), mined for her gifts, but always kept in check, lest her power create chaos in the ordered masculine universe.

In just the same way, the personal forms of goddess were usually seen as subservient to the dominant masculine divinity. Of course, the western Abrahamic religions denied any feminine form of transcendent Godhead. Eastern traditions did and do honor Goddesses, but usually as consorts, intercessors or hidden protectors to be called on in times of crisis, and placated for boons. Even in polytheistic traditions, Goddess was rarely given equal status to the masculine Godhead.

So, one of the great projects of our time has been the re-claiming of feminine divinity. This has happened partly through the work of feminist scholars like Marija Giambutas, Ann Baring, and Jules Cashford, who uncovered evidence of goddess worship from all over ancient Europe and the Middle East. Just as important, though, is the permission that modern feminism has given individual women to unleash our own intuitive connection to Goddess. As women have begun to emerge politically and socially, we've also begun trusting our own emerging wisdom about the sacred feminine. Not only are we learning to tune into our own bodies and to the natural world, but also to the radical philosophical implications of sacred feminism. Even more important, we're recognizing through direct experience that Goddess can't be confined to the physical or even the imaginal world because she is the very impulse of life itself.

The great Goddess traditions of tantric Hinduism were among the few to understand this. These traditions recognized that Reality is both still and dynamic, both witness and actor. And, most radically, they understood that creativity and power are inherent properties of the sacred feminine. Because they saw Reality as equally God and Goddess, they were able to recognize the sacred feminine not simply the field of masculine creativity, but as the actual impulse and power of creation itself.

Sacred feminine spirituality offers a particularly brilliant view of the connection between the One Goddess, and the forms in which we can relate to her. A true lover of the sacred feminine can see her as Mary AND Kali, as Gaia AND Isis. Most radically, she can be experienced as your own Self—both your individual quirky personal self, and as your one divine Self. As several writers tell us in these pages, we can see her as the all-pervading life-force, as our feminine organs, as our interior silence, as our thrusting joy, as our sexuality and our insights, as the bark on a tree or the flower that blooms after the rain, as the energy of water and, equally, as the energy of fire. She can appear as a statue of the Madonna, or as a coiling snake, as a deep moonlit ocean or as your sister, or your mother, or your lover—even as your bitchy boss. We can find her in anything because she is everything. Ultimately, we find her in our own awareness as well as in our bodies and hearts.

This book invites us to range through the fertile terrain of Goddess experience, Goddess visionary insight, and Goddess energy. Enjoy the testimony in these pages. Dip into different poems, contemplate the prose pieces. Notice the insights that arise in you, the recognitions, even the energetic feel that comes through these pages. Try reading it in a meditative mood, in small bites, so that each piece can set off its own contemplation for you. May this lovely book be an inspiration in your journey through the wide pathways of the Goddess's world!

Sally Kempton
Author of *Awakening Shakti:
The Transformative Power of
the Goddesses of Yoga*

Women's stories are as powerful, inspiring, and terrifying as the goddess herself. And in fact, these are the stories of the goddess. As women, we know her because we are her. Each woman, no matter how powerless she might feel, is a cell within her vast form, an embodiment of her essence, and each woman's story is a chapter in the biography of the sacred feminine.

Jalaja Bonheim

Introduction
Catherine L. Schweig

T here are as many ways to relate to the Goddess as there are sparkling stars decorating the night's sky. But are they stars, or jasmine flowers, adorning the black tresses of the Goddess herself? Ancient narratives overflow with such rich goddess imagery. The endless colors and shapes, textures and flavors stretching across cultures and traditions for millennia, harken back to humanity's inextricable link to the Divine Feminine. Regardless of the particulars of new and emerging historical contexts—intent on pinpointing the degrees to which our ancestors were Goddess-oriented—this rich and wonderful diversity reflects the ability of the Goddess to reveal herself in as many unique and individual ways as there are beating hearts on our planet. For the most meaningful path to trace is the one She makes into our own lives.

I grew up in a valley partially rimmed by the elegant silhouette of a sleeping goddess. At her side is the crouched outline of the warrior she was meant to wed: now a 17,900-foot live volcano. The oral traditions of my childhood tell of Ixta, the Nahua princess, who would have become empress of the valley had she not slipped into a seemingly eternal sleep while Popo was away at battle. When Popo returned and saw Ixta's lifeless body, he fell to his knees beside her, immobilized with grief.

To this day whenever Mexico's live volcano, Popocatepetl, spews smoke and ash into the sky, it is said that it's because his heart is still aflame for Ixta, aching for her to rise into her reign. Instead, the sleeping Goddess rests beneath a blanket of snow. I remember watching her sparkle in the sun on the way to school wondering what our lives would be like if Goddess Ixta ever woke up and became empress.

The words in this anthology speak not only of the shared anticipation for the Goddess to come into her reign, but also illuminate a Goddess who never really left us: a Goddess whom many of us have come to know quite intimately over the course of our lives. For, as these writings reflect, the goddess often reveals herself in phases and cycles that magically match our own. As we grow, so do our conversations with the Goddess, informed by stages of development and awareness that deepen from childhood, through puberty, and into our adulthood, while simultaneously sustaining the intuitive wisdom that's been drawing us to her all along. As we awaken, we shake the sleeping Goddess, so that her voice becomes more audible to us.

This diving into dialogue with the Goddess then becomes a mirror of our own selves and the magnificent multitudes we each contain. As we identify with specific energies and qualities that we ascribe to the Goddess, we verily give ourselves permission to locate these same energies and qualities within our own beings and express them in the world around us. The personal essays and poems that follow emphatically weave such tales of transformation and empowerment, as voices of women from around the world unite to pay a very raw and real tribute to a Goddess who has not only been roused from her sleep, but who has also shared very dynamic relationships with each of the authors.

We enrich our individual relationships with the Goddess the more we discard any limiting preconceptions and open ourselves up to her vastness. For the Goddess has presented herself in fancy folklore as both fierce and gentle, dark and light, old and young, seductress and virgin. She's worn silks and jewels, feathers and leaves, sung like an angel and screeched like a banshee. She's been wet and dry, fertile and barren, maidservant and queen. Consequently, we allow our experiences of the Goddess to simultaneously incorporate such typically opposing extremes. Like a circle from which nothing is excluded, it's not uncommon for today's personal portraits of the Goddess to blend multicultural interpretations of her essence, and to fluctuate according to each of our unique visions. This feminine fluidity flows through the pages of this volume, often intersecting where the streams of the author's sundry expressions converge.

In organizing the voices that flowed into this project, three primary Goddesses emerged: "The Eternal Goddess," "The Mythical Goddess" and "The Goddess Within," although some of the pieces could have easily fit into two, or even all three themes, for the Goddess is not easily contained.

The Eternal Goddess is she whom the authors have found in the moon and stars overhead, tracing the curvaceous paths of orbiting planets, tucked into the magnificent darkness. Held within her cosmic womb we experience her as a nurturing presence—lush and fecund—bursting with fruits and flowers, silhouetted in awe-inspiring mountainous and volcanic ranges. She is the familiar Earth below us, grass between our toes, water that sustains our cells and the rhythmic seasonal shifts syncopating with the drums of our own hearts. Protective and primal, she reverberates with timelessness—her archetypal cords connecting our cultures—as we've all suckled at her breasts, and known the warmth of her lap.

The Mythical Goddess is depicted herein with many specific faces and forms, arms and wings, halos and horns. Her personhood is synonymous with her sacred qualities, her magical stories: enchanting narratives that have woven themselves into the emotional fabrics of humanity for ages. We devotedly carve her out of stone, fashion her out of wood or clay and luxuriously adorn her with garlands, gems and metals. She is the muse of ritual and offerings unfolding in remote caves and urban temples alike, both modern and ancestral. She sings and screams, dances and fights, dying and being reborn over and over again, mesmerizing us from one generation to the next. Calling her by many names we summon her, pray to her, converse with her and have even heard her calling out our names as well, since time immemorial.

The Goddess Within is she whom the authors described as swirling in our psyche, rooted in our core, dwelling as part of our own essence, flowing through our veins. She inhabits the energetic fluctuations in our bodies, the inner revolutions of our cycles and the deep feminine characteristics that empower us. Compass of our introspective voyages, we experience her as intuitive wisdom, enhanced receptivity, the ebb and flow of our very beings. Her oceanic juices flavor our identities as much as sauntering through her mystical deserts do. The line where she ends and we begin just an elusive pinstripe upon the velvety garments that beautifully define us.

The Nahua mythos of my girlhood anticipates a time in which Ixta shakes the Earth and Popocatepetl blows smoke announcing the awakening of the Goddess, whose frozen blanket of snow begins to melt. Together, the feminine and masculine energies would interact lovingly, ushering in a new era: the era of the Empress, in which all would thrive. As this book comes to fruition, the interpreter of omens in me can't resist linking this ancient Aztec tale with the recent earthquakes and volcanic explosions shaking my childhood geography, spewing lava and melting snow: just another sign that perhaps Ixta's coronation is indeed imminent, that the dormant is stirring, that the Goddess rules. May the words that follow become an invitation to explore your own relationship to the Goddess and Her overdue reign!

If there is to be a future, it will wear
a crown of feminine design.

Sri Aurobindo

The Eternal Goddess

The Goddess is the Eternal Mother, the sacred and sensual vessel of creation and transformation. She is the one who births and transmutes; She is the portal between worlds, through which all life flows. When she is dishonored, all of life suffers, for She births all creation. When She is honored, all of life thrives.

Sara Sophia Eiseman

Vitamin G: The Goddess Deficiency
Lucy H. Pearce

Women are the unknown in patriarchal medicine. We are the Other. Our cyclical bodies are bemusing, confusing, frustrating to the logical requirements of Western doctoring.

What is wrong with you? This question is asked almost as much as the statement, *There's nothing wrong with you.* But there is. You know there is. Deep down you know that something is very wrong. But what?

We are told how malnourished many of us are in terms of vitamins and minerals: we are getting obese on empty calories, whilst our bodies and minds are getting sick due to a lack of basic nutrients from highly processed foods made from fruits, vegetables, and grains grown in depleted soils. Our souls are suffering similarly. I believe that we are dying for want of an essential nutrient. One as yet undiscovered by patriarchal science: Vitamin G, for goddess.

Take your pot of supplements and check the back—there you have Vitamins A through E. When you give birth your baby is rushed a shot of Vitamin K. But did any doctor give you what you most needed as your body was weak with PMS, as your soul flagged with exhaustion after giving birth? I'm guessing not.

After millennia of being reared in a spiritual context that teaches and acknowledges only the masculine, that deifies the male and shames the feminine and female, we are all—women and men—severely lacking vitamin G: the goddess, the divine feminine. Its effects are visible everywhere:

> The destruction of natural habitats
> The medicalization of birth
> The inequality of the status of women
> The rise of rampant and destructive capitalism

Like treating any micronutrient imbalance, it requires raising the intake of only the one lacking. So if patriarchal religion and culture were Vitamin C—we are all able to access plenty via fortified orange juice, supplements and even sweets available at any shop. We are immersed in it. Whereas vitamin G is a rare commodity in our culture, it must be carefully sought out. A little like placenta encapsulation (itself a form of imbibing the sacred feminine) you have to seek it out, privately, with strange looks—no doctor or supermarket is going to be providing you with it knowingly. You have to go under the radar.

Vitamin G is usually self-administered through pleasure, and charting, and walks in nature, movement, song and stillness: through painting, and chocolate, and orgasms, and dancing in the rain... or via a women's circle or rite of passage ceremony.

For those who are still Goddess resistant, all this naked dancing in the moonlight is a strange prospect.

Many wonder why the obsession with the Goddess. Why are all these crazy women collecting images of goddesses and talking about their menstrual cycles and worshipping the moon and getting their knickers in a knot about women's rights and retelling ancient myths? Why can't they just... not? It's making us uncomfortable.

I would say it is an active, unconscious rebalancing for souls starved of her for generations, on pain of death. Women will probably always be more drawn to the Goddess as she reflects and represents their natures and bodies and experiences more. For men, she represents the mother, lover and muse and the opposite of themselves. The energies of divine masculine and feminine are both needed, but we are treating a pandemic, a chronic and pathological imbalance. The doses needed are high and frequent as we come back into balance, into full health.

We are sick from imbibing the Father, Son, and Holy Ghost our whole lives, from inhabiting patriarchy, learning to objectify and hate our bodies, learning to undervalue ourselves and be in competition with other women. We are sick of living in a rhythm alien to us and in a culture so hostile to life and love.

On discovering the missing piece of the puzzle, the lacking element—the Goddess vitamin—we start to feel ourselves coming back to life and health, to our native power and strength. Physically, emotionally, mentally, creatively and spiritually we feel ourselves fully nourished perhaps for the first time in our adult lives, or our whole existence! As we begin to incorporate different ways of being and knowing—cyclical wisdom—into our daily lives, it feels like we have finally come home to ourselves. After a lifetime of soul and body sickness, we begin to regularly ingest the Goddess vitamin again: here to save us all from essential malnourishment.

They Say

Kimberly DuBoise

They say you speak through symbols—
maybe even circumstance—
but I would rather you speak to me
through the eyes and hands of a child
or a beloved's familiar smile.
A poet can capture on paper only a fraction
of your words, and a song
can only hold so many notes;
what I'm trying to say is that you
have no equal—
there is no substitute for you!
I am calling you here, asking you to be present
in my life. Now.
In this moment.
Fill the corner of my universe with your light!
Your presence heals,
it renews and restores,
transforming us back into our
intended glory.
Our divine Self, emanating from You,
emerges and shines with radiance
once we turn our face
toward the light and the love
that You are.
I am facing you. Ready for what you have to say.

A Call to The Great Mother

Lauren Love

Goddess: Magic, Myth & Mystery!
Who is She?
Who are you Great Mother?
I call out to She: Please speak to me.

I open myself to be a vessel for your words to flow, to use my body, my mind and soul. As the cycles turn and the seasons shift, I wait patiently for your voice to be freed. I am here, open and free for She to enter me.

You have initiated me; spun burning roses upon my crown, sent the Raven to be perched on my shoulder, ignited the dragon within my womb. You've sent symbols and messages through the ethers of time, witnessed and translated in order to find. I want to know who you are, beyond the symbolism and beneath the signs. To see you, to feel you: all of you!

Goddess, reveal yourself, touch me with your sacred hand, show me your fingers of love streaming across the ancient land. We are waiting for you to rise, rise within us, rise within us all.

She who is the rhythm of the Universe, the beat of the Earth, the flow of the Land: Embrace all within your sacred web of creation! Cauldron of life, Creatrix of nature, we call to you to come home Mother. Please forgive us for the depths of our destruction. We call you back with wide-open arms.

We Love you Great Mother, Please, come Home.

Divine

Reshma Mirchandani

Empowerment belies the varicose undertaking
of minimalist thinking.

How do we rise above the cautionary tale?
The flailing dance between power and humility
sets us below the need of what we ought to believe.

The power to be more than just a deed or a sleeve
or a mountain's reprieve
commands us to own our own skin
beyond the eye of what spins.

The divine dwells in the midst of the abyss
where we still find life in the mix
of fear and reproach from stilted growth.

There's more to the world than that little girl
with wide-eyed wonder and twirls
around an amber frenzy of twilight and heat.

If she doesn't leap to the bounds of dollars and sounds
of idols and clowns,

her pouch of cosmos dust will be quite enough.

Aligning Ourselves with the Paradigm of the Goddess

Theresa C. Dintino

For me, the Goddess is not a female replacement for a male God in the sky watching over us, judging our actions, making sure we get it right—or else! Rather, the Goddess is a way of life, the womb-like container that holds us, as well as the field of potentiality within that container which we arise out of and dissipate back into again and again, as seeds into the Earth. The fecund ground of her being nourishes, protects and feeds us as we, with our experiences, which include death, feed her. She *is* Source, the All. Gods live *within* her. This is the paradigm of the Goddess.

The paradigm (worldview) of the Goddess is a way of being, a reality different and other than the current mechanistic paradigm (life as machine) we live in, (also referred to as the patriarchy), and yet the one revealed more and more through biology, physics, biochemistry, and cosmology. This reality has also been confirmed to me through divinations I have done in my time as an initiated diviner.

When I first encountered the paradigm of the Goddess in the books of Marija Gimbutas—wherein she catalogues the archaeological remains of Paleolithic and Neolithic cultures of powerful ancient women long forgotten, *ancient sisters through time*—I felt in my body the *memory* of a time when we truly lived in this way, in alignment with the paradigm of the Goddess.

I have spent the past thirty years trying to listen to that memory. I believe if we can match the energetic vibration of that time and paradigm, remember it deep in our bones, it could find its place once again in current reality. That faint echo has been my guide and teacher. It has been an interesting, challenging, and exciting journey.

The paradigm of the Goddess is a oneness, an interconnectedness, a wholeness which contains individual components that are each sovereign wholes while simultaneously one. The Goddess is source energy, source of all, womb that contains and holds all.

8

We are embedded within her consciousness, generated and sustained by it. She *is* the holographic universe of which we are part and parcel—holograms—as well as the vastness at once.

I have seen this reality in divinations as a vast woven web of networks alive and interacting. Each life and consciousness helps create this web. Through our choices and actions, we add to this complex tapestry, co-creating and participating with all the dimensional realms. She is the multi-dimensional loom onto which our individual experiences create the texture and patterns of reality. In this web we are always connected, have instant access to all and are never truly separate.

We are at once the vastness and the reduced focused lens, the wholeness and the small individual stories, ourselves, and she. Light is the thread that weaves form into the thick and ever-present darkness. Consciousness is the needle with which we stitch our designs. It is ineffably beautiful to look upon. Elegant genius.

All the lives we live and timelines we create are etched as memory onto this holographic body. This we access through divination where we are able to interact and collaborate with this grand, ever-present now.

This is the truth of our existence.

This reality is also encountered by scientists working in the realm of what we call the "quantum." According to biochemist and geneticist Mae-Wan Ho, PhD., the universe (Goddess) is a live organism, a contained system that operates the same way on the quantum and macrophase scales. Ho's descriptions of the reality she observed in her time as a biochemist match what I call the paradigm of the Goddess. In her conclusions from years of work, I find confirmation. In my divinations, it is *this* actuality I meet and am taught more about. It is important to me that certain disciplines of science are meeting and describing this same reality. We must allow ourselves to integrate this back into our psyches and try to live according to this knowing once again.

Within this system, Ho states: "Each and every player, the tiniest molecule not withstanding, is improvising spontaneously and freely, yet keeping in tune and in step with the whole. There is no conductor, no choreographer, the organism is creating and recreating herself afresh with each passing moment." This is a perfect description of the paradigm of the Goddess.

However, in divination I am also shown another "reality" a false "grid" around the Earth which most of us are currently plugged into which is at odds with this other truth. We waste our precious time and energy by participating with it. Literally, I am shown our energy lines being siphoned off into this alternate grid around the planet, which wishes only to feed itself. And it does not matter if you are male or female.

We have created this grid with our own beliefs. No one imposed this on us. We believe life is a machine. We believe we are machines lacking interiority or having existence or relationships beyond the 3D. We channel our energies into systems that support this belief, powering it further.

And yet the truth is, we are alive within an alive cosmos.

This self-destructive myth we are currently living by is killing the planet. We must change this in order for Gaia to survive and humans to thrive.

To live inside the paradigm of the Goddess once again is to change the way we conceive of ourselves. We need to *change our minds* about what we believe to be true; teach ourselves out of the mechanistic worldview we are inculcated into. (When I say "we," I speak of those living in the west or within the construct of the Western World. Indigenous mind still lives in what I call the paradigm of the Goddess. They never left it.)

If we believed and knew ourselves to be nurtured and sustained, by the paradigm of the Goddess, we would live in an immeasurably different reality.

We only need to believe the truth of reality rather than the false one; we don't really need to change anything but our minds.

The power to do this is encoded into women's ovaries, which create and carry eggs. We carry this pattern of wholeness, this paradigm of the Goddess within us. We must go inside to find it and reactivate it. Women are encouraged to spend time meditating on the power of their ovaries, moving through the spiral patterns held there and learning what they have to say. (If you do not have physical ovaries, simply work with the energetic ones.) The power held there is immense, more that anyone would believe. We are the Goddess and we carry the Goddess within us. We must seize it and bring it for the greatest good of all. Only we can do this now. We hold the key.

Hysterium

Tiffany Lazic

A note appeared on a sign in my head
"The new path is old, forgotten and dead.
It has held sway for 2,000 years
Nourished by guzzling millions of tears."

Our Goddesses used to stride over the land
With power and grace, an indomitable band.
'Til, to hostile forces, triumph was dealt.
The Goddesses snared in a chastity belt.

Shackled, subverted, entangled in lies,
Their vision still glowered with low, cast-down eyes.
For 2,000 years held under the boot,
Their open reception unleashing the coup.

The land has been raped, the water a-foul.
A rumbling deep, Earth-wise rises to howl.
The power of phallus unable to rise,
The usurping energy shrivels and sighs.

For 2,000 years, it guarded the land.
For 2,000 years, blood flowed from its hand.
For 2,000 years, Nature has been abhorred.
For 2,000 years, deep wounds have been scored.

Now lying facedown in the dirt and the muck
The Goddesses growl "We don't give a f***".
Like Boudicca driving her Destiny fore,
Their shackles are grasped and thrown to the floor.

Cursed chastity belt, the final to fall,
Bares womb wide open to birth it all.

No more the phallic stabbing thrum,
But warm pulse of Hysterium.

No more the murder of our kin.
No more the charge of grievous sin.
No more our bodies deemed unclean.
No more heard wailing, tortured keen.

Our Goddesses stand tall and proud
While men and women form a crowd.
A new day promises to dawn
Where all are viewed as pure and strong.

The land respected as Divine,
"Hold Love for all," now read the sign,
"With honor, grace, and dignity
To balance Land, and Sky and Sea."

The quiet crowd begins to part.
One Goddess, shining, stands apart.
The final act of freedom-grasp
Sheilagh bestows the vulvic-clasp.

And sword is finally laid down.
The Cup instead reveals the Crown.
Hysterium, the guiding light
Gifting us all with unveiled Sight.

The Water Goddess
Jazzalina Garcia

As a child, I always loved water. Wherever there was water, I was in it. Loving to swim or play, and there I would stay for hours on end, deeply connected in joyous harmony.

Later in my adult years, I seemed to lose that beautiful and precious connection. I got lost in another world, far removed, even becoming a little fearful of the sea, and what was hidden in those watery depths. This, I now know, was a fear I had developed of my own depths and what lay hidden within the unconscious realms within.

Several years ago I stopped myself in my tracks, and decided it was time to swim in those feared depths of myself. To find the answers to questions that sprang from the well of my own discord. So I bravely began a very important and life-changing journey of Self-discovery: To reclaim the lost and disconnected parts of myself and fully realize the truth of who I am.

At the very beginning of this journey, I sat in deep meditations in complete solitude, really connecting to the core of my being. At first I encountered some resistance because of the unknown that had kept me locked down in fear for so many years, but I sat with that, lovingly, knowing that my authentic Self would safely guide me through.

The first meditation revealed the biggest truth I needed to hear: that I was suppressing the Feminine energy within me quite strongly and had been for a long time. She had been carrying the weight of everything I couldn't deal with or rejected. So overwhelmed with this deep revelation and connection, I broke down in tears. I was speaking to my soul: The Feminine and Masculine aspects of myself in deep conversation. Her voice was at last being witnessed in conscious presence. She was hurt, angry, laying in darkness holding all the painful memories and fragmented parts of my soul.

I broke down and apologized for my selfish behavior, even though it was in complete innocence, for we are programmed to be this way. To be split from the whole. To reject opposites that seem negative. Rewarded for being happy or good, punished for the bad.

Yet, when in truth, reality embraces it all, knowing that all things need to be in balance, working as one. As such, it was such a relief to finally reunite with the whole of myself: To be embraced by the Feminine, feel her love once more, her forgiveness. To reassure her that I would always listen, be with her, in everything. That she no longer needed to carry the pain alone. I would no longer run from it, as hard as that may be at times. I thanked her for her strength, her wisdom and courage, and felt a deep sense of oneness return, though I knew this was only the beginning.

The days and weeks that followed brought deep shifts within me. All self-deprecating thoughts ceased. I saw that now the Feminine aspect of myself had been seen, honored and reunited with. Her anger had ceased, and I was no longer hearing her punishing voice in my mind.

I also found myself drawn to water once more. I had discovered a beautiful stream nearby in some ancient woodland, and would go and sit in stillness and meditation there, really connecting with the water. Listening to her with my whole being. Hearing her wisdom, learning from her, embracing her fully, and feeling the flow within.

I came to fully realize the true power and nature of the Goddess through water. For me, her Divine form is embodied in the water—water being the opposite to fire, which I see as the Divine Masculine energy. And there is an alchemic balance between the two, which is the true nature of Love, which is *our* true nature. Where the real source of light and bliss are found. The two touching in harmony and at One in an infinite dance.

As the years have passed, my relationship with the Water Goddess has deepened. I often have tremendously powerful connections with her, as if channeling her Divine spirit through me, which is both immensely healing and joyful, making me feel blessed beyond all expression. I recently went into a very deep experience with her. It felt like I was touching and being touched by her essence at the purest and deepest level, as if our hearts were one and spoke the same language. I began to channel her voice, singing ancient melodies in a language I had never heard but felt I knew. I felt baptized by her touch, as she washed over my skin. My soul felt renewed and deeply in love with the beauty of the Goddess who gives all to those open to receive. I was then gifted an amazing journey that took me through a complete re-birth into the true Self, embracing not only the Goddess's energy, but being taken into the Father's arms, where innocence was restored, and I was carried back down to earth in the form of water, to be reborn into the earthly body, then becoming a tree—the symbol of Self. I can only describe the whole experience as an incredible gift from the Goddess.

As my journey continues with the Water Goddess, I continue to heal on all levels, reconnecting to the wholeness that I am. It's not always easy, and sometimes I feel disconnect in myself as more distortions present themselves: things I have carried in those watery depths for so long, some for lifetimes. But water remains the constant. That keeps me in heart and balance. That soothes and cleanses and shows me who I am. Her wisdom is my guiding light, her love ever present and flowing. I stay connected in many ways. The Goddess is ever present. One just has to sit and be with her, to listen and become, because she is within us, and we within her.

You Came Looking For Mother

Gloria D. Gonsalves

All the water in rivers and oceans
all the trees standing tall and free
all the blooms on ground and air,

I was there.

I was the water gushing from the womb
I was the food while bleeding on moss
I was the epiphany of the mother goddess.

My grounds are sacred venues of life
there you have been alive than above
as you crawled, walked and stumbled.

I let you trample life on my surfaces
I let you plant and reap as you please
I let you drill me to depths of miseries.

There is a reason you came looking
nothing surges ahead without living
coz' nobody knows you like a mother.

Awaken in deference to your soul and spirit
for without them you are a covenant of putrid.
Grant me your worship in all forms of life.
Do you want your mother goddess again?

Misunderstandings of a Selfless Soul

Grace Gabriela Puskas

Poor, sweet goddess
how many times are you abused for your kindness,
or responded to with hatred from denial and misguidance?
How many times is your genuineness met with distortion,
with illusion and confusion from a world drenched in caution?
Where others are made to believe a soul so real and true
could not possibly be real, so they judge and ridicule you.

Sweet, true goddess,
how many people have you helped with your words,
with your time and your patience and your desire to serve?
How many people have had blessings from your being,
yet still think it right to take without seeing?
Do they see the real you, do they even believe,
when their own selfish nature just feels for their own needs?
How many are happy to continuously take
without giving back the universal way?
And how many you have sacrificed for and dedicated your life
have showed up for you in times of real strife?

Poor, suffering goddess,
how many have been there for you when in need,
when it is not only you giving but in need of someone real?
Someone who truly cares for your sadness or pain,
beings who will selflessly sacrifice their needs to put you first,
without gain?
Are there many of these people, or is it solely you;
are you the only selfless one misunderstood and seen right through?

* * *

In a modern world it is hard to find a soul so real and true,
who truly sees a stranger's needs as completely equal to you;
a spirit who will happily sacrifice a certain comfort, luxury or need,
and will overlook another's actions, even if rooted in greed.
Yet this no longer works dear goddess, not any more in this dimension,
yes—be real, be love and kind, and always maintain your compassion!
But the time has come where you are the one that matters most
in this game,
by respecting and loving yourself above all others, you will allow
true love to reign.
This is truth,
this is love;
this is power.

Family Kitchen

(ritual for the gathering and healing of a blended family)
Jacqueline Davis

Cinnamon spirits rise from piecrust
like mist over evening fields where a barge
and an island—say Avalon—
might drift till morning.

You lean against my shoulders:
Lancelot as he longed to be,
at home in a cluttered kitchen,
watching the last glow of orange
through five o'clock windows.

On days like this, I imagine cauldrons
and food blessed under stars
by women who danced moonlight
into the earth of fresh-sown fields,
wind in their hair a thousand years ago;

In the dawn, men raise sickles,
chanting as they reap:
> "Corn and grain! Corn and grain!
> What's cut down shall grow again!
> Hoof and Horn! Hoof and horn!
> What has died shall be reborn!"

Recipes come as easily as spells:
> Peas green, onions white,
> wild rice to cure lice,
> three strands of willow hair
> and something wet
> from the river's edge
> to secure a lover's pledge;

carrot-moons and parsley root,
three sprigs of lavender
before the owl's hoot...

Vegetables roll and churn as I stir
like words from a favorite story.

As cheese melts into biscuits,
I hear my grandmother's
thick-heeled shoes clunking
over kitchen floorboards.
She's serving roast and dumplings,
heavy with gravy,
some Sunday before I was born.

You turn to me as our children
come back muddy and laughing
from the pumpkin-haunted compost
where they've dumped vegetable peels
over sunken Halloween faces,
their rivalry on hold until the card game
and popcorn an hour after supper.

A last light from the window flushes
each cheek as we sit at a table grown large
and round as a harvest moon.

Tonight the swamp witch and the wounded king
at the edge of our story rest—jilted Alayne
lies down with Arthur; they make a bed
of the barge that's floated
far from battles and promises to return.

Launch

Kai Coggin

l am balancing
on a spinning planet,
holding myself down
to the ground with my toes clenched,
ready to spring into the abyss of space,
the wonderful blackness pinpricked with stars,
ready to rejoin everything that l see as light
from down here.

Dance of Venus

Mumtaz Layla Sodha

A fter the following words flowed through me I discovered that there is indeed a dance dedicated to Venus: the orbiting pattern Venus makes around the Earth, which geometrically portrays a 5-petalled rose. Every eight years, when the Earth and Venus 'kiss' to form another petal, Venus presents the same face to the Earth. The dance of the planets: their retrograde motions, synodic periods, distance and orbits present us with patterns that resonate with their essence, and ours. The patterns of Venus' dance are extremely beautiful: those of a heart and a rose. They reveal the essence of Venus in her role as celestial guardian of love and beauty to us here on Earth.

You say it is You who pulls at my Heart
It is You I yearn for night and day
That emptiness yearning to be filled with Your presence
It is You that my body—my breath—calls to even in my sleep
That unending longing that each of my cells radiates
As if repeating some ancient mantra.

You say it is You, So where are You?
I only hear your voice yet my body is still cold
I cannot feel your breath upon my skin
Or your wild passionate embrace calming my bewildered heart
I still feel that raging fire within my Soul
That threatens to devour me whole.

I feel a thirst that cannot be quenched by all the water on this plane
A yearning so deep that even by peeling each layer of my skin to my bones
I cannot feel any greater pain.
My Beloved, what am I to do?
What am I to do?
Then, She speaks:

"You are to Dance! Even till your last breath of yearning
you are to Dance!
Allow your yearning to devour you
Allow it to consume every part of you
Like a ravenous dragon eating your being from the inside out
And when each part of you is overcome with longing for Me
You will no longer be you, for each of your cells will be filled
with Me
Then, my love, there will be no You, only Venus!
Only Love."

The Goddess of Everything
Taya Malakian

There are as many faces of the Goddess as there are stars in the sky. At times she comes to me gently as Quan Yin or Mother Mary, and other times she storms in as Kali. She has been Tara to me for many, many years and has appeared as a hundred other faces as well: Durga, Freya, Hathor, White Buffalo Woman, Lilith, Hecate, Aphrodite/Venus, Persephone and more. Sometimes I have been frustrated at how She wouldn't pick a face and stick with it. She was always changing, always dancing and then I realized that this was exactly what She should be doing...

She appears in all things, in the blossoms that call our hearts to expand in the Spring, in the sultry heat of Summer that makes us long to disrobe and share our beauty, in the letting go and decay of Fall, and in the barren desolation of Winter. Yet even then there is life still teaming beneath the surface.

I see Her in the waxing and waning dance of the moon. I see Her in the changing tides, in the rushing river near my home that we call Yuba where I saw Her as Vajrayogini, and in the sky where She dances without a name.

I see Her in the fire that burns for ceremony. I see Her holding court at my altar as a witness and support in my trials and triumphs on the journey of awakening.

I feel most connected to Her when I am in Her stomping grounds: the outdoors, where She would come to me as Artemis when I was a young maiden. And even when I am inside, I feel her as Hestia guiding the way I maintain my home and as I engage in quiet reflection when home alone.

When I look to the world, I see Her waking from her slumber as Women gather to march in protest of the hyper-masculine and privileged governance that is trying to establish its throne. She is being remembered.

In college, I discovered how deeply the Ancients worshiped Her. I saw for the first time images of Goddesses with fertile figures, paintings of Her that captured rites in Her honor, and yet it was a deep remembrance in my bones. Here was a treasure trove of loveliness, of childbearing grittiness, of nurturing and abundance, of death and destruction. She was here, hiding in the deeper layers of the soil, or discarded as not important to the search for the roots of humanity. Yet she was also, meant to be found, and even casting her out couldn't keep her away. When I saw how the Ancients cared for Her and how close She was to them I cried and ached, longing for that kind of devotion and connection in this modern world.

I found Her as I dove deeper into the study and practice of Buddhism. I connected with a Tibetan Buddhist center focused on the Practices of Red Tara, who teaches us how to transmute our earthly love into true compassion and bliss. I also found Quan Yin; even in a hall with 1,000 Buddhas, she was there, pervasive among them.

I found Her in yoga. There is irony in that a once masculine-dominated practice has come to the West to meet with intensely devoted female practitioners who outnumber the men by far.

It was through yoga practice that I was introduced to the wisdom of the Vedic Sages, who saw all of Nature, where all things manifest as the Goddess, and beneath Her, the Divine Masculine as an all-encompassing consciousness. I love this intercourse of consciousness and matter, masculine and feminine that takes place in every cell, every atom, and in all of time and space. This idea was introduced to me through Tibetan Buddhism, but it became a living reality through the practice of yoga, or union: union with the Divine, and union of yin and yang: the feminine and the masculine.

So She... She is everything. Every face is Her face and yet She wouldn't exist without the Masculine. Let us hold them both, with their differences and strengths, and honor them as One: The Goddess of Everything with her All-Pervading Partner.

The Hunt

Shannon Crossman

We go out
Hunting God
As if She were
Some sort of
Quarry
Hiding behind
blinds, we call
out in false
imitations
attempting to
lure Her close.
That we might
bag Her to
turn trophy
hanging
on proud display.
Far better
for us to go
stalking the continents
of our interiors,
dark jungles
that they are...
Willingly they divulge
what was true
all along.
The only game
worth hunting
is your Self.

With Love, Gaia
Rachel Lyon

You have stripped me
Tearing away my dignity
Polluting me
Drowning out my voice
With the squeezing of your dirty, greedy hands

Children huddled round, prodding a worm
And throwing stones
You didn't know
They didn't feel
the hurt
Or see me bleed

You clawed my back
And pushed me down
Into acid ridden seas
Corroding my shell

I thought you would want me back by now
To raise me from my watery grave
To remember my name
I thought you would remember the love
That I wrote in the sky as a rainbow
That I sprinkled in the sky as stars
To guide you home
These breadcrumbs I have left for you
To return and love me again

But you have forgotten
I was your first breath and I will be your last
That I carried you
And held you through the wind and darkness

And gave you shelter
Here in my heart

As my light goes out so does yours and I will say to you
Sing to you on the winds that brush your ear
That like the flame from a candle
A drop from the ocean
A mother to her child
You are me and I am you
Entwined
And I forgive you
And hope that one day your light
Will shine

If I am Eternal Goddess, It is My One Large Eternal Eye that Leads You into the Night

Amy Leona Havin

Traveling through the American West, amongst days flying past riverbeds, praying to red rocks, and resting at edges of desolate highways and dry grass meadow... I found a compass, pointing towards my true North. It asked me to take fragments of memory, mind, winds, and language to create a capsule of eternal time, tethering me back to these moments. To look back on and remember, that a Goddess is made, in the moments when she is born. This poem was written in fits of madness, in between road-novel dreams, in cars running across the deserts, and in the shadows of God-carved mountains. This poem was written amidst times of freedom, ultimate autonomy, rebellion, and with howls to the wind. This poem was written to remind me of my majesty, and of brighter days, and will surely come again.

Watch the power lines swing, monument to monument,
across the open pear-blue of the storm-beam sky.
The more rain touching the desert dust light,
those tentacles of celestial force,
the brighter and more birthed the Earth Mother.

While her shaded peak, resting in the distance,
paves with the flashes of lightning beyond its
Southern facing mound—
it is sweet Desert Rock
pale brown, armor taupe, waiting
as it has for one thousand years
in the West
for the light fall.

As we drive in the very center of the roadway,
I feel no fear. Hopping my bare-naked toes
over rocks through the window,
body calloused with the dirt-stained pads,
avoiding serpent holes in the side of the small butter highway
with pebbles made of glass.

Pinch-fills of brush and plant and wild root
are pulled quickly with the taut twist of toe knuckle.
If they are meant to come, they will break.
If they do not break, then they refuse to come.

A ripe sage grind, isolating both smell and hardened paintbrush
on a humid-coast afternoon, speaks in tongues for the last parts
of dusk.
Shattering medicinal herbs to the haven highway-lands of the
often un-traveled
and weary-minded medicinal warrior. Making for us skies of
sheet metal,
spears of lightning, and the legendary roads—
kept dirty with the remnants of flash flood legacy.

Like the light-dry Mother Mountain
emerging to the East in a film of Utah dust.
I cry for her and the buffalo air
and I promise I will behave
for the night fall
the unraveling road
and the snaking lonely byway
Laying aside these highway pebbles

Poor rocks
Poor stones
Poor junk

Discarded junk left out and ground up by the days,
hidden sweet amongst the hooves and roots.
Oh, cousins!
Who flourish here in the tending solitude, Teach me your
freedoms!

Learn me not your words but your wildness!
Spread far and grow wide to the horizon line, running like children,
following me down to the bottom byline.
It is you I am never without!
It is you for whom I count the bare musk patches,
serpent-hike mounds, and prairie rodent dens
fetching pieces of me to feed to their vacant beds.

For in these days, I step foot from unearned liberty,
slick as sage and scented Dill,
thick as the morning air and more ancient...

The sleeping eyes and Albatross mind,
The Eternal Priestess of my sanctity,
becomes greedy for my ever-restless blood.
The crunch underneath my feet, stricken by sandal flay
and rising with the lift of weight,
now activated by vibrational lungs and exhilarated
by the devastating honesty of
Nature's True Howl.

I gaze into the speckled hills, an immense exposition
of humanity hurdling back in the impossible exhale of misuse.
The wind howls. The bowl howls. I howl to the wind.
And to the sky and to the desert wolves—
perfect coyotes bantering folklore across the coarse
and arid landscape.

I will not re-live this day.

Tomorrow, the Eastern lightning storm touches
down, connecting us to the Intrinsic Mother
flashing light up anew this Western Wall
and we will ride into town
ill with future
lightning on our backs.

Sedona

Anu Mahadev

red, red sandstone, soft, sedimentary
rock, i hold in my porous palm and

i crumble to feldspar, quartz, into,
the concealed crevices of my skin—

a cliff of bones. this textured aquifer
i am, its lithic liesegang band, percolating

liquid flowing into a powdered body of sand.
once i emerged from this earth, writhing,

warped, water in my hollow words. not
for me lush lava, landslide spilling

into the valley. woman, *vama, stree,* i curve
to the river. i am the bridge on that river,

i am the tilted truss supporting the bridge,
its unwieldy body. i am the planet, i am

the seed planted in my womb. this is blood
that won't wash away, that threads the timelines

of your being. that plunders, pillages lands
that are my own bread basket, my goblet of wine.

i am these that nourish you, nurture you,
i am the nameless nomad whose map you

follow, for there is no beginning, no end.

we must return to the place where the red rocks rise.

Chasing Fairies

BethAnne Kapansky Wright

She is the first mountain
I ever climbed.

8 years old,
I think I can,
one foot in front of the other,
because I didn't want to quit
and thought I heard
the songs of fairies
hidden in her gardens
and went in chase.

Today
magenta mixed with
mahogany erase—
muddy treks
and white flecks
and tundra collects
and hides 10,000 Who's
in its specks—
I almost hear their
joyous noise
over the thunks of my
earth slick steps.

This mountain,
she hides
all her mysteries
in her wrinkles
and her lines,
blink—
and you will miss them,
her portals to the divine.

Things unseen,
yet still alive,
worlds within worlds
on her face reside,
and just as I did
way back when,
I go in chase of
the invisible,
mystical,
unfathomable,
foreseeable—
(if you have the eyes)

Her magic waits in
the in-betweens,
earth's kaleidoscope
of rhymes.

The Jewish Goddess Never Left

Nanci Bern

I t is Shabbat. The antique candlesticks are newly polished. I light some cedar. Tendrils of fragrant smoke swirl. Each week when I reach for my candles, I reach through time. My fingers become coated with the light that was, the light that is, and the light to come.

I draw the flame to my eyes three times then reach upward to call my Neshamah, the part of the soul that only comes for this holy time. I lower my hands in thanks. The room becomes a garden of time and dreams where so many have done this and as so many will after me.

Did the women before me feel me as their future, as I feel them as my past?

I close my eyes while I chant: "Shekinah, Divine Feminine, Goddess, who are you to me?"

How does my Jewish—my Earth Reverence path—soul inhale this presence? How does my heart exhale it back to my world? Surprisingly, it is the still space between my breaths that resonates most deeply with the answer.

I walk into this quiet place. It is verdant with spirit.

The ground is laced with shimmering greenery. The light is dappled by whispers of prayer and song, incantation and musing. They hold me while I sway with their rhythms.

A tree with bark as old as the earth's first breath stands in the center. Ancient smiles are embossed in its woodsy skin. Tears, like sap, have run through its ridged bark.

This must be the Asherah Tree. This is the Goddess of my Jewish spiritual lineage that, although of Canaanite origins, Jewish women worshipped. She has never left us, but she has been transformed. I imagine Asherah and Lilith, who is a sacred force as well, watching me.

I first met Asherah, my first Divine Feminine awareness, when I was four and knew that hugging trees was a holy act. I met Lilith when I was seven as I walked the spiral descent of the indoor garage staircase of our synagogue that at the end became a succah. This deep and holy cement path is as profound to me today as it was then.

I met the earth and the mother, and knew there was more to my Jewish path than what we were being taught. It was easy for me to form a bond to Nature as this was the closest I had to a physical connection to what I knew was present, but was not being shown.

My eyes continue up along Asherah's bark. Our secrets, prayers, song and souls that she held in her crags and valleys begin to smooth. The 'crotch' of her tree, where the trunk separates, is draped in blue velvet like those that cover the Bimah (a podium in synagogues where the Torah is read). On it rests a Torah scroll. The Divine Feminine, our Goddess, has been hidden, made invisible.

The branches that grow from this point, gracefully reach toward the clouds. They are enveloped in a grey mist that looks like smoky flames of thought. Hebrew letters float within them.

And I know what the Jewish Goddess means to me. My connection to her is earth bound and heaven high. She is my first relationship to spirit. She is the power that shines above and below. She is my power within. She is the womb of containment and the great birther.

But, she is also the wounded. She is the pain of the earth and the pain of women. Her anguish sears my soul. Asherah has become a vapor of presence in the growth of male-centered Judaism.

Because patriarchal Judaism does not render divinity into visual representation, we cannot see Her. We express holiness in thought, social and environmental action, spiritual practice and relationship to Nature. The divine feminine consciousness that is within our minds and hearts is now the body of the Goddess.

When this shift happened, Asherah, Asarte, The Queen of Heaven, became the feminine force called the Shekinah which means 'to dwell within.' But within what? Within the earth, within ourselves and each other. She dwells within the mystical structures, such as the Tree of Life. The feminine waters of creation— called the Nukva—is redolent with Asherah's spirit as well. Our Goddess is all of these and more. She resides in time and memory, our bodies and the earth. The Queen of Heaven is on earth by the way we walk and love in the world.

She lives through the woman-centered Jewish customs and tales that cling with ferocious love. Even the prophet Jeremiah knew that women's ceremony, such as the celebration of Rosh Chodesh—the new moon—that was connected to the Goddess, could not be dissolved by the ink of this next phase of male dominated Judaic development. He knew of Asherah and knew she had to stay. She, the Shekinah, dwells within this. Solomon's temple even had an Asherah Tree. There are more places that 'She' can be found and we must go there.

I believe that our ancestors are also our Goddesses. We can conjure their forms and their acts: Rachel, who sat on her Goddess states to protect them, Miriam who beat her timbral at the sea, Hulda the prophet, Deborah the judge, Bruriah the scholar, Judith the warrior, Esther the brave, Ruth the faithful.

But as much as my hair tingles with Her breath—that is the wind when I spin on the fields of celebration—as much as I embrace this Goddess in my hands as I garden; I also love many aspects of Judaism that developed after Asherah was forced mute and the Shekinah became her latter counterpart.

There is beauty in the heady constructs of Jewish thought, even though it's patriarchal in its nature. I love the study, the denseness of Jewish theology that is its own holy path. There is spirit in the letters I saw dancing their own sacredness in the tree. I do that dance as well.

We need these two paths to become one. We need to be embodied with our faith, turn our questions into the boldness of form that breathes with presence and passion.

Tikkun Olam—the fixing of the world—is a prime Jewish concept. Whether it is considered in the interior world of spirituality, or the outward push of justice; a wrong must be addressed.

In order for the rectification of the Divine Feminine to occur, we must first apprehend the depth of the sacred. We, all, must put ourselves in front of the Goddess. I long to sit with Rachel and hold her holy statues while we pray. I will journey through the centuries to do this. I invite you to come with me.

I hear a rustle to my left at the roots of her tree from which I have not moved. A hand, textured of the earth, reaches upward. It beckons me to kneel. Flowers spiral along her fingers. Stones and gems from the deep beneath of ground illuminate her palm. This is the Goddess calling me, calling us back to Her.

She places her hand on my head. I feel her blessing flow through me. Tears of the great pain, and the great joy of the cosmic, cascade from my heart. I pray that they will be a spirit calling to those whose time it is to celebrate Her again.

The space between my breaths that called me to Asherah is a liminal space. It is the in-between of the truth of what the cosmic Feminine is and what Judaism is today. This is where we can evoke the Goddess of our origin and the Shekinah of today. We can join them together and invoke our relationship to Her.

I look to the day when an Asherah tree is planted in synagogue gardens as a matter of course. I feel the stones within the ground begin to reveal themselves, like the frost heaves that reach upward, as if they feel my urge of quest for healing and wholeness. She will not stay silent. She will reveal her gems again and we will give Her glorious presence.

She Shakes Our Tree

Rhea Ruth Aitken

She is shaking us:
Those of us that hear her.
Shaking us by the roots
Until all that has hung on too long,
All that is decaying and broken
Falls to the ground,
Gone from our magnificent branches
To be forever reclaimed in lost time.
Then she shakes us some more,
Gently teasing the last from our clutches
Until we are free from our hurts, our fears
And our moldy decaying paradigms.
Until we see the light filtering through,
Feel new emotions and reach skywards
Open armed to new life.
And so we sow our own newness
Bud and then flower
Beautifully, powerfully
Into our glorious wild selves.
Our roots grow further, strong and deep,
Anchored into She: our Mother,
Drawing from her wisdom, her potent love.
We are stable within them
Yet able to bend and flex with the winds of life,
Our buds and blooms in tact
Our beauty ever present.
We will not be burdened by
That which is not worthy to hang from our branches
Or sit amidst our bright blossoms
Or add heavy weight to our free flowing limbs.
We honor ourselves,
Keep bright our boundaries.
We feel her, we are her.

We rise ever upward
And as trees in the forests we unite
Creating sacred spaces,
Rooting together, growing together
In a place of mindful peace,
Perfectly balanced light and shade
And heart centered unity,
Where all women may be present
And hear her as we do.

The Reclamation of Woman

Louise Whotton

We have long reached a time when it is necessary for Woman/ Womyn to be reclaimed, for tearing apart the myths and stories that have persisted in our dualistic, masculine world. It is now the time for metamorphosis, as we transition from history to *her*story.

In the prevailing history, women/womyn's voices have been taken, captured and contained within a shell, used against her to squash her dreams and quell the sounds tumbling from between her lips. Yet our power is in our togetherness, our unity: we must join together, encircle the whole of what is, embrace the cycles and enter the dark so that we may come into the light of understanding. We will then enter a new phase in his(her)story, rewritten in a new language, for womyn conceives the world and dances from her dreams. She transcends the phallocentric view of the world claimed by men, in which she has been the object of attack; the snake that haunts her dreams invokes the domination of the male, the phallic, the freedom of the Gorgon. Yet Medusa conquers the phallic, reclaiming it, powerfully forging a whole, and a myth emerges: the sorceress, the hysteric, the lunatic, the witch.

Womyn's power sparks fear, for she uses her body to conjure: this conjuring takes place in the cauldron, the pot, the womb of the mother. Within this hollow, hallowed space, she forms speech, she writes, she forms symbols and metaphors of the unknown yet knowing. By way of Water and Earth she comes whole, splaying herself out, blooming fully, she is the gushing of the waves, the saltiness of the sea. She follows the cycles of the moon, once a month embodying the moon's power and sway, to fill, full, lull, let go, push out, release... the waves break upon the sand. Like the sounds of the waves in a seashell, there is always more to listen for. She lets it all encompass her, flow through her until it is written or vocalized; her body is her anchor.

Yet her dance of desire has long been cast aside. Dualism serves to strengthen the myth that has kept women subjugated, as this binary always implies a dominant entity and an Other, one side reigning supreme; womyn have been oppressed and rejected time and again. The rage and sickness of our foremothers have spilled into the present. The witches and wild womyn were burned for their passions and wants: to help and to heal, to use their bodies, nature, cycles and the moon. It is now time to reject masculine notions of sex and desire, to lock the box of the phallocentric system and throw away the key. It is time to recapture our intuition, which has had to remain in hiding for too long, to allow the erotic to burst forth like the red-hot spray of a volcano.

Shaken and disorientated, womyn will take back what is hers; it is time. She will start to creep forward and then push herself out to the world with force. Like breathing, the newly heard sounds will become nature, stories passed on from the foremothers, around the fires, the red tents, in grandmothers' kitchens. There will be an understanding of more than language, long the domain of his-story and which rejects feeling and knowing, while fostering separation.

For womyn is whole; she is not half of our current dualistic hierarchy. Once this wholeness manifests, woman will have full access to her body and desire, but she must first relearn to use them in her own, empowered way; she must deconstruct them in order to begin anew. She must also recover what has been pushed out and ostracized, that which has always transcended the old systems; in doing so, she will also become liberated, while eschewing what has been divided to create wholeness, which has always been circular, the past and the future forever present. We must, too, assume a bisexuality, a mixing of the sexes, a circle formed from disparate parts. To achieve this, it is imperative that we find our powers of articulation seek balance and disentangle the myths that have served the masculine hierarchy.

In doing so, we come to a new view of knowledge and truth, one that rejects the hierarchy's notions of the linear, forever pushing forward in one direction: we must reject masculinity, rationality, the running forward at a cheetah's pace ignoring the power and blaze of the wheel spiralling in the belly of the feminine. It is in this way that we can all find and experience the truth that will set us free.

What we need is nothing short of a revolution: we must create and favour the vortex that envelops all; we must forge a world with no boundaries, and our entire way of knowing must be re-imagined.

It is imperative that we turn to the red string of fate that binds us, becoming entangled, even as each side battles to pull away. Imagine a world in which each side is free to flee yet bound out of love rather than necessity and the spectre of death.

In the new unity, two sides become one, pulling together, never still, always spinning, dancing the feminine spiral to the depths.

She Is
Julia W. Prentice

She is the feathery tracing of lichen
On the gnarled tree trunk
Do not scrape her off to find new wood

She is the patina of age on old silver
Chased and whorled and slightly rainbow
Resist the temptation to polish her off

She is fine china, webbed with tiny cracks
The fissures part of her inheritance
Blending stark pattern into lovely

She could be a crystal goblet
So worn with use there's spider webs
Etched on glass once bright, now dim

Go out into the woods to find her
Seat yourself on lichen-covered throne
Glowing moss green and gold foil

Dine on fine china, eat with old silver,
Drink from goblet and inherit
Her ancient beauty and wisdom

Toast to the Goddess without and within

Communion

Shawndra Miller

I am like you; I crave connection with the sacred.
So often I feel lost and buffeted in a fractious world. Like you, I
find the news of the day unbearable.

Then I contact an invisible realm that nourishes me, steadies
me. It's a deep, dark, womanly, watery place. Maybe you've been
there too, in your quietest moments.

Sitting one morning, longing to join with something beyond
myself, I see a tree. Majestic, with rounded canopy and massive
trunk—it's a tree of storybooks and watercolors, on the edge of
a meadow, distant from me. The distance collapses and I touch
its rough bark. I hold its trunk. Energy runs through my body as
it runs through the tree's, flowing into the roots through my feet.

Have you ever made such contact?

If you have, whether in dreams or visions or skin-to-bark
contact, you might have sensed Tree's immense gentle ponderous
power as I do.

I can feel its tree kin drawing near in spirit, too: A vast com-
munity of trees, breathing.

I feel the lungs of the planet expand and contract in my body,
as I breathe with them: A breathing like saying grace at table, in a
circle of beloveds.

I travel deeper and deeper, and wider, and connect with
threads of fungal mycelia spreading in all directions. Soon I stand
on roots that brace like tendons along the soil surface, and then I
move from embracing the trunk to crouching between the roots,
palms touching these sinewy conduits. I sink farther into the soil
with each breath. I expand *outward outward outward*, through the
mycelium chain that snakes everywhere, runs through everything,
even through oceans. Until finally I embrace the whole world.

I hold Her. In contact with the whole of Gaia, I feel my inhale
draw in all the way through the planet. On the exhale, energy
moves through my palms into the tree's roots. And I weep. I take

responsibility. This earth so beloved, so beleaguered. I say my prayers for it, and feel the weight of responsibility.

Nothing to be done, I am everything; I am all—and so much of it painful. I hold that too.

To be in communion with all—carrying every hurting bit of life inside me. Is that what I signed on for, when I came here empathic? Just now, the burden feels light, yet so imperative.

I am willing, I say silently.

I know that I hold fracking-tainted water and raped wombs and acid-tinged oceans. The thinned mollusk shells, the death of corals. More than that: I am the rapist and the drunkard and the shooter and the corporate titan, the complicit woman, the abusive father, the grieving grandmother, the benumbed youth.

I am the heart and the head and the genitals of the world.

I am all of it. It is myself. Gaia equals Shawndra. Shawndra equals Gaia. Gaia holds all; Shawndra holds all. (Perhaps you know this oneness too.)

And to know it is to weep, and to say, *I love you, Please forgive me, Thank you, I take full responsibility for all of it,*
all of it.

Empress
BethAnne Kapansky Wright

Empress. Earth Mother. The Divine Feminine.
78 cards in the tarot deck. And only one the Giver of Life.

Each time I turn her over; I stretch out my heart, reach forth, and
see the love in the face of a creased, old friend.

She makes me think about what it would be to twine butterflies
through my hair, soar high into the sky, transcend the lines that
keep us in this space. Learn that the secret to flying is found when
we yield, contract, shrink, turn in—so we can spin cocoons of
shadow selves and seek our dark moon's face. Then emerge with
the light, when day breaks from night, taking flight towards the
bright on new wings of truth and grace.

She tells me to shrug off the world as I knew it.
To lay down my armor and layers and shields, to sit naked in her gaze.
To go to the sacred in nature, to talk to the river, to sit by the trees
and re-realize, repurpose, reclaim my *life given, love driven, soul
dwelling place.*

78 cards in the tarot deck. And only one the Giver of Life.
The Empress, she smiles with knowing eyes. An archetype of
abundance; matriarchy; wise. She reminds me to gently spiral
within, run free with the wind, learn the secrets of wing and hoof
and fin, to trust myself down to my heart depths inside—

That there awaits my divine.

She

Irma Aguilar-Olivas

A loveliness unfolds
of time nor distance measured
in archived mystic verses
the ancient poets treasured

Behold, the Sacred Feminine
with her enigmatic glance
in the universe of oneness
SHE exudes deliverance

draped in loving-kindness
illumined wisdom and bejeweled reverence
the Divine One of consciousness
unearthing our benevolence

creative life-force drenched with sacredness
SHE heals and nurtures, delivering our sustenance
within our heart's where peace we keep
in the quiet space of love SHE stays
with the wounded souls of a soul that weeps

and her eyes with tears of sadness bleed
when lives are lost to wars and greed
if only where the angels stray
enlightened paths our thoughts may seek

"...bliss, is in the air you breathe"
her eternal loving verses speak
abundant heart of wisdom may
unveil the clues to answers reaped

"...bliss, is in the air you breathe"
in the sacred songs of devotion prayed
from the whispers of the wind we greet
her essence embodied in journey's deep

SHE whispers in a voice as sweet—
"...bliss, is in the air you breathe"

Natura, The Green Goddess
Pegi Eyers

In my creative work, renewing my relationship with *The Sacred* begins with encounters in the wild, and quiet "earth blessings" that recognize the magic of *Natura, the Green Goddess* flowing through the land. I am filled with gratitude for nature's abundance, and for the sights, sounds, smells, tastes and textures that are nature's enchantment and joy. And after a time of deep listening, I come to rest in the arms of the *Green Goddess*, a heart-filled space of unconditional love. For the very essence of *Natura* is love! Love is found everywhere in nature—and love is the vibratory field for the plant kingdom, the nurturing power of the Feminine, the kinship of the creatures, and the elements such as water.

And yet, in our human-centric society there is a huge lack of knowledge regarding the natural world, and the human/nature separation is painfully extreme. In my own work as a writer and educator, *Natura* has led me to guide other women to find their own eco-selves, and to be at home again in the *Sacred Circle*. The love of the land has always been central to our most cherished dreams and memories, and if we delve far enough below the surface of the modern mechanistic overlay, we find that *Natura* has been waiting patiently for us to return! It may seem that urbanized humanity has given up on the Earth, but the *Green Goddess*—with her harmonic intelligence and great heart—has not given up on us.

Loving the *Green Goddess* with a fierce devotion may mean that we view the damage being done to *Natura* as attacks on our own family and kinship groups. The despair and rage we feel as witnesses to terracide, animal exploitation and the everyday disrespect for the land can be channeled into creating awareness, resistance efforts, the *Earth Rights* movement, and by rejecting the destructive values of Empire. When we open our hearts to *Natura* in our thoughts, words, actions and cultural life we will find sacred purpose in the co-creation of an earth-honoring commons, and restore much-needed balance. Our re-enchantment with the *Green Goddess* is essential for devoting ourselves to rewilding, eco-activism, environmental healing and earth remediation in these times of massive change.

Today, our task is to bond with the land, to revere *Natura* again as our Ancestors did, and to see ourselves as part of this thin and fragile biosphere, *Our Earth*, the source of all life and our spiritual home. The beauty and timelessness of *Ancestral Wisdom* is an unstoppable force, as recovering indigenous mind becomes the goal for all people. We have eternal access to a deep well of earth-emergent knowing, the divine pattern lives on in the DNA, and *Natura* sustains us with everlasting healing and restoration. Our journey arrives full circle in a surprising paradox, with the revival of *Ancestral Mind* becoming the simultaneous path from past to future, future to past and back again! All things arise again in perennial growth, and the essence of the *Green Goddess* is "veriditas," or the irreducible principle that the souls of all beings are blessed with renewal and rebirth. Remaining in place as a timeless, thriving and ever-rejuvenating mystery, the unfailing themes of abundant life continue to manifest even as we move into an unpredictable future.

We are all *Children of the Earth*, and at the heart of our seeking is a veiled desire to be reunited with our perennial family, the other-than-human world. Educating ourselves about the landforms, plants, trees, creatures and seasonal patterns in our bioregion is a life-long undertaking, and in the meantime, there is so much to love in the natural world. Graceful horizon lines, stalwart trees, soft breezes shaking the seed pods, animal tracks, sinewy snake tracings, endless variations in leaf and stone, patterns in sprout and decay, feathered shade and bird song all speak to the senses, and we know the charm and delight of the creatures endlessly calling their names. Are we listening? What are they telling us?

When we hear the voices of *Earth Community*, we are transfixed by the many distinct expressions of beauty, spirit, and practicality. Taking time for these important encounters and experiencing "timeless time" is how we revere *Natura*, and with love, express the earth-honoring ceremonies that align us with the intrinsic balance of natural law. Both the macrocosm and microcosm of the *Green Goddess* are sentient in countless unique ways, and *Her* response to your biophilia, reverence and positive energy will bring the greatest surprises and joy.

Blessing and being blessed, today I join with my *Earth Sisters* everywhere in the songs, chants and practices that celebrate *Natura,* and the powerful forces of unconditional love that empower all of our partnerships in *Earth Community*. Each moment is a gift of vitality and joy, and when we align with the magic of the *Green Goddess* we are in harmony with the world, and *The Sacred* that dwells in ourselves, all beings and the natural world.

the dancing girl of mohenjo-daro
Anu Mahadev

it's my day out at the art museum. the freer and sackler galleries.
the bronze statue of the dancing girl mocks me. one hand

on her hip, she challenges me to guess her name.
real girl in the indus valley civilization sits on a parapet,

red sandstone on her skin, watches the tulsi plant in the center
of the courtyard. raindrops drench her, ricochet off the bricks.

jasmine petals flutter from her hair onto her tanned fingers.
bangles size up her arms, urgency clasps them to jangling wrists.

clouds wring last drops of monsoon, sponge it clean. water
mixes with the muddy gully, carves ravines on her wet palms.

she's filled with dread. that time again, a hall of strangers.

for silver anklets to pound uneven sandy floors. for the sun
to sink into the indus. she must talk often to herself, in the paddy

fields, scrawl her name in the mud. she must hang her hopes
on mango branches, dream of escape. she must braid her hair

with fireflies, that hiss in the crypt of her heart. yet she stands,
feminine, sacred — here, now. i examine my own wrists, my feet

encased in casual converse sneakers. is she a goddess?
a slave? whom does she love? does she live, like me, for love?

On Fire

Cynthia Blank

For once, I want to be the wild kind,
burning, sending smoke into the air.

I want to be worshipped like a golden idol,
trailing the scent of incense and myrrh.

I want to shake the sun awake,
to feel endless crowds reaching up for me.

I want them to use me, to touch me
with the light of heaven, to fling me away
wrapped in flaming sheets.

I want to feel more than standing in this quiet
Tel Aviv suburb, in absolute control.
I want to be what's really on fire.

But I'm not burning, I know, I'm not burning.
There is no fire; I've been all-wrong.

Awoke

Tammy Takahashi

In the blessed
little ones
scampering up
great hills
of mirth and joy
innocent, still,
of shadows
and dangerous
places,
lighting a
thousand suns
with their
laughter,
rooted in
deep
knowing

In the
growing ones
pulsing with
the love of
Mother
bleeding
compassion
like the most
luminous stars
of vast timeless
night, as old
stories soar to the
watchful moon
guiding

For she
is the ground
that kisses and
nurtures the
wounds we
bear and
the ones that
will still
come
home

For she
is the sister
rustling the
root of us,
rising up
through the
tree of us
cradling the
generations
of us
the seeds of
our eternal
bloom.

The Divine Goddess
Healing Our Planet Through Compassion
Anita Neilson

T he spirit of the Goddess can be heard in the ether as we expe-
rience a rebalancing of planetary energies. Sometimes she
whispers a gentle lullaby on the breeze; other times, her rage carves
through the air like a fierce harridan, dispersing old energy to make
way for the new. I believe we all strive for a state of harmony in our
lives—mental, physical, spiritual and emotional—in our desire to
thrive. When I used to accidentally cut myself as a child, it was to
my earthly mother that I ran. She would comfort me in her arms,
cleanse the wound, and then apply a healing salve before sending
me out again into the world renewed, rejuvenated and uplifted.

However, it is to my spiritual Mother that I turn again and
again when I'm confronted with life's challenges. She resides in my
inner wisdom, my growing intuition and my longing to show love
and kindness to all forms of life. She goes by many names, such
as Divine Goddess, Sacred Feminine, Moon Goddess and Divine
Mother, among others. I watch her influence sweep its healing
balm across the planet, knitting together our self-inflicted wounds
of egotism, intolerance, judgment and ignorance.

Goddess energy has been growing in recent months and years
to counterbalance the ego-bound mores of intolerance, distrust
and fear, which have pervaded our dealings with each other over
the centuries. More and more, we are awakening to what is truly
needed now: a rising of the vibration of love and compassion in
our hearts.

A beautiful consequence of this inner healing journey as we
seek balance is that we are then better-equipped to spread love
and kindness to those around us. We can lead by example not
judgment; we can be guided by intuition not fear; we can accept
difference with delight, not suspicion.

This is The Goddess in action!

This is the Divine Feminine I see slowly yet firmly infiltrating the establishments of power on Earth, and with this soft invasion comes a turnaround in business and politics, proffering new, positive ways of working together. These are not evident at first glance. A level of discernment is needed to stop and evaluate what we see and hear. Let's actively seek out these pearls of grace which encircle the planet yet have for so long been obscured by our ingrained habits of ignorance and desire.

There are so many Goddess pearls I feel are brightening our lives, right in our midst. There is, for example, the rise of social enterprises, not-for-profit companies and cooperatives, true examples of the Divine Feminine energies of compassion, intuitive wisdom and understanding, here merged with business acumen for everyone's gain. They often employ the traditionally shunned, such as the homeless, ex-criminals and the long-term unemployed, with profits oriented to the future wellbeing of the company, employees, local areas and charitable causes as everyone is paid a wage affording them a decent standard of living. Social enterprises imbue a sense of purpose in their employees, awakening in them a willingness to serve others for the good of all, to work not solely for individual personal gain but also the collectivity.

We have also seen the rise in positive journalism coupled with new university courses fit for the 21st century, such as those in Holistic Science, Ecology and Spirituality, and Sustainable Horticulture. These are further examples of the Sacred Feminine energies continuing to restore balance to all areas of society. The old norms in the media and education sectors are being worn down as intolerance cedes to a growing level of compassion and connectivity among the populace.

Increasingly, we are witnessing women assuming a valued place on company boards and in politics, enabling a shift in decision-making at the top levels of society, and carving a path toward new ways of cooperative governance. We only have to look at the rising number of powerful female world leaders in countries such as Germany, Croatia, Switzerland, the UK, Malta and many more, to see the Goddess energy evolving and changing our world, ushering in a new paradigm of peaceful resolution to conflict.

On a more grassroots level, we can observe the resurgence of crafts and traditional ways of doing things: a return home. The 'old' (feminine) wisdom of healing herbs, of make-do and mend, of making our own clothes and growing our own food—these have all recently made the transition to mainstream institutions, homes and new businesses after half a century of being consigned to the peripheries. Society has now embraced these creative skills and attributes, and the values they represent.

Another truly powerful, and very personal way in which I encounter the Goddess energy vibration is in meditation, periods of reflection or prayer, and while I write. I hear her matter-of-fact voice answering my questions with the tolerance and patience of a heart full of love. I see her reflection in each full moon, as she simultaneously pulls me skyward and inward, and I experience her love as a blossoming in the heart chakra—once closed off through sorrow, fear and negativity—but now infused with ever-new joy, contentment and positivity. Old habits and blockages are dissolved in the nectar of her love. She is forgiving, understanding, kind and compassionate. She imbues me with her wisdom and love for all that is, seen and unseen. She is my saving grace, and she joins me to you!

As kindred spirits and carriers of the light, we can make it our sacred duty to share this divine Goddess energy with others. Let us warm to her spirit in every cell of our being by following our inner wisdom, listening to our growing intuition, and showing love and kindness to all life—for that is the enduring and eternal legacy of the Sacred Feminine.

My Goddess Stamps Her Feet

Alise Versella

Remember child
You were born from me
Earthbound boy blue from the cord
Blue like the sky that turns black only for the stars
You were birthed from my womb
Earth Mother Gaia expelled the titans from her uterus
Uranus
Didn't know how to tame such chaos

She knows how to reign in chaos
She knows how to breathe underwater so as not to drown
She gave up the air from her lungs so you would scream
That first holy sound
How dare you quiet her?

This silence is not golden
This silence is the beginning rumblings of the plates
Before the earth starts shattering
I am shattering
Laying waste the poppy fields like Kali
Because I see the poetry in destruction
The same gods you pray to unleashed their floods
So pray to your gods now for communion

This is holy uprising
This is for all the wars fought against my body
For all the witches burned, this is the pyre for my transforming
Stand transfixed by the wings of my metamorphosis

My menstrual blood can revitalize that rotted apple twisted
by the vine
Like Isis brought Osiris back to life

Can't you see the flesh turn red?
Like the red of Lilith's lips when she sipped Dionysus' wine

They want you to lie
Cover up the talon tears of the canvas, paint the colors porcelain white
God forbid you decide
To rage and rage and cry
Like Mother Nature swirls her brush through the storm
and decides to paint a hurricane
Deracinates the roots they dug into your vertebrae
Like a willow tree you bend and bend

I want holy revelation
For the way my body curves
I want you to see the temple I built from my words

What if god were a woman
Would you still fight for her cross with a bullet?
Or would you plant those strewn poppy seeds
Would you create something from the smoke and ash
of the buildings you see crumbling
Would you string a ribbon 'round the May Day pole,
Fix a maiden with a flower crown
Before our mothers turn to crones

Would you even notice if the moonlight dimmed
and the owl's feathers prevented him
From flying?

'Cause Child it feels a lot like dying.

Goddess of Alchemy

Zoe Michael

Introduce me to your demons
I'll acknowledge them as angels
Showcase your fiercest entities
I'll face them and stay faithful
Feed me with your rejection
Inject me with your fears
I will taste the sweetest love
Ingesting beauty from each tear
Surface my deepest shames
Throw me into a maze of guilt
I'll reconstruct my layers
And build a worthy web of silk
Pollute me with your poison
Tie me up in low vibrations
I'll have immunity to every toxin
Shedding skin to new creation
Dig your knife in deeper
Suffocate me with your chains
I'll solidify my total core
Find a pleasure from the pain
Remind me of my dark days
Taunt me with my scars
The cracks beneath my surface
Will shine through like the stars
Present to me a pot of weeds
I'll grow a garden of flowers
Hand to me a simple stone
I'll create a crystal tower
Every abusive word you say
Will allow me deeper expression
The manipulating games you play
Are vital to my progression
Encase me in a dark cocoon

I'll emerge a butterfly
I'll spend my whole life transforming
As old stories within me die
For every fear breathed into me
I will transmute into pure love
I am a universal ray of light
I am peace on the wings of a dove
Whatever you choose to give to me
I'll receive with gratitude
For I am a Goddess of alchemy
A divine creation of amplitude

The Flame of a Candle

Jasmine Kang

Through the night,
With the light
Of the stars from above,
She guided the heavens,
The earth and all,
Protecting the land,
And giving radiance
To the horizon
With the beams
Of the sun at dawn.

The child was dazzled by Her manifestations.
"Victory be thine forever and always."
And the words echoed through,
Carried by the zephyrs that swam
Through the clouds and the blue
Of the night sky.

Here I was, but yesterday, Her child.
Though aged, the dweller of my heart
Was yet the same,
Yet the same.

Reverence

Beate Sigriddaughter

Do you want me to kneel? I whispered.

No, she said, that's mostly for men,
they like the ritual to reinforce
their image of importance.
Normally I never even notice.

I need you at my level, here,
where wheat stalks rise
in robes of braided seed, and poppy
petals, graceful as Japanese silk,
life liquid plump in their veins,
substance of butterfly wings, rose
buds, glossy feathers, and foxes
splitting the snow like lighting.

Consider the choreography
of lilies in the field:
don't you know that you are gods?

Then help me, please, to translate this
magnificence into a language
even men agree to understand.

The Mythical Goddess

Every era has its goddesses. Sometimes, as in civilizations gone by, they are welcomed and honored. Sometimes they are in hiding, ignored or marginalized. Sometimes, as in recent times, they are even burned alive at the stake. But the true goddess spirit cannot be destroyed or excised from civilization because it is "Shechinah"—the feminine presence of the Divine, which is eternal. In the Jewish tradition, the Shechinah is thought to be "in exile." It is believed she will return when the peoples of the earth honor the godliness of one another and of all of creation, and thus the era of lasting peace will begin. May this become the era that is known as Shechinah's Return From Exile. Let us open our arms to welcome her return. May we— her earth daughters—be blessed with Shechinah wisdom, strength and compassion to help make the world whole and holy.

Ruth Broyde Sharone

Creation Myth
Alise Versella

I was raised on myth.

On the story of a man and the woman pulled from his rib
It wasn't until I was older that I learned of another named Lilith
The truth of beauty and power hidden in what was labeled sin

Of a girl, so at one with her own darkness, she followed Hades down
And ruled among the underground with a pomegranate crown

Of a huntress of the night who ran unclothed below the moon
To lead a wild hunt against the men who would devour her if
they could

That same moon pulls at my bones until my legs crack
at the kneecaps
And I run unhinged alongside Artemis and her wolves
I think young girls are like werewolves: we grow so much our
bones hurt, we grow a pelt of hair; the moon makes our belly's
bloat with insatiable hunger, famished. And when our hearts
break we bleed. Every month we bleed. The salt we weep is the
same as the waves the moon pulls from the sea.

I am a daughter of the moon
A body made of stars
A galaxy burning brightly like the fires lit in our hearts
One day I will burn up
My soot will become mulch for the dirt
While my heart is weighed against the feathers of the crows
that follow me home

Home is where I was raised to believe I'm magic
After all I can create life from within
Look closely and you can still see

The knobs of bone that used to grow
Faerie wings between my vertebrae
These crystals vibrate with my touch
I manifest spells that work passed my lips
Like whispered prayer
Like poetry

I am creating a new story
Where witches burned are goddesses and god is just a man
who asked politely to hold my hand.

Beware

Joan McNerney

If you touch Medusa
her serpents will wrap
themselves around you.
She soars through water
with giant wings gold fins.
Hundreds of snakes
crawling from her head.

Some long to be near
Medusa to hear her hissing
lisping songs forgetful.
She can suck blood from
throats coiling minds
past infinity before
they breathe again.

West Ended

Jaclyn Piudik

The tail of a swirl becomes insidious at times
                    the rip in a sweater, an ending.

In search of largess—a sign
                    of daggers
            broken shimmers
        proven ghosts
laminate tales of daughterhood

Elizabethan angels—irrelevant as last week's gossip
shag haircuts, contradiction at the dinner table.

Saint Anthony loiters at the corner store
finds pearls in the trash can
and on Muir Avenue, we relive
theology through the dance

in the parting of the sofa,
refuge from the icicle gallery,
city of beard and bone.

Echoes of skin unfold
with the gradualness of seven sunsets

blood knots fall from their bindings,
clochards of the upper realm.

I look for Persephone and she is silent now.

The World Behind the World

Shavawn M. Berry

T he veil between life and death is especially thin each autumn. *We shed one skin to reveal another.*

Fall is the time when we travel into darkness. In Greek mythology, this time of year is represented by Persephone's kidnapping to the underworld. The perfect maiden, Persephone is stolen by Hades—the god of the underworld—to be his queen. After her departure, light is non-existent. Crops wither and die.

Demeter—Persephone's mother—is beside herself with grief. She's responsible for the fecundity and fertility of the planet. She stops doing her job, obsessed by her quest to find her daughter.

The world plunges into darkness, starvation.

Eventually, Demeter is told where Persephone's been taken, and seeks her return. Hades—ever the trickster—promises to return her, but only if she's eaten no food while secreted away. He tricks Persephone into taking a pomegranate seed into her mouth, and some of its juice passes her lips. Because of his duplicity, she cannot leave the underworld permanently. Hades uses this to ensure her return to him every fall. Persephone is released for half the year (spring and summer) and in bondage for half the year (fall and winter).

In a time largely disconnected from ritual and symbolism, we tend to avoid preparing ourselves spiritually for handling our own *dance with darkness.* We might not see the lesson embedded in this myth regarding the balance of life and death, light and darkness, but *we should.*

We must learn to realize that everything is not as it seems.

What I love about this myth is the fact that growth is happening even during times when everything feels dead. The frozen ground may seem fallow, but rain, snow, and the passage of time, work to enliven the soil, so that when it's time to turn it in the Spring, it is rich, moist, and fecund.

Demeter cannot make things grow in soil that never rests. We cannot continue to advance if we never take any down time. This tale speaks directly to our real need for balance in our lives.

We tend to overlook whatever aspects of life that we take for granted.

When Persephone is snatched away, we realize she embodied pure, wild beauty. Without her, the world is a dark place. However, unless we understand the ephemeral nature of beauty, and treat it reverently, the sting of its loss will always surprise us.

Everything cycles through birth, aging, sickness and death. Everything. The child becomes a maiden. The maiden becomes a mother. The mother becomes a matriarch. The matriarch becomes a grandmother and the cycle repeats.

We peer at the invisible world behind the world, perplexed.

These days I often think about the invisible aspects of life. Things I know exist: Atomic particles and single-celled amoeba. Angels and guides. Ethereal beings. Travel at the speed of light.

I think about *the world behind the world*: The one that exists underneath the sheen of this reality. The one that pulses with life and light, unlike the fear-based, terrified, freak show we believe is the 'only reality' there is.

Persephone's story regarding the *appearance* of a *disappearance* illustrates our energetic reality perfectly. Just because something appears to be gone, doesn't mean that it is.

Death is, in fact, a human construct. So is life, if you think about it.

We are pulsating masses of energy, and energy cannot be destroyed. It can change form, but it cannot disappear. Therefore, death is simply a part of the life cycle that leads, eventually, to a birth or rebirth, depending on your viewpoint.

Each fall, we find ourselves at the precipice of the dark night. Persephone—the energy she represents—has been spirited away. Leaves scatter and gardens rot. The days grow shorter making light harder to find. We long to sleep, but when we do, our dreams are filled with frightening encounters with animal totems, dead relatives, and the steaming skins we've only recently shed.

We are raw and newly born.

We need to hibernate. Our translucent skin glows as we burrow deeply into the cave-like rooms of our unconscious. Before a new world can be born, we must un-tether our souls from the one we're living in.

Unfortunately, some folks cannot traverse the chasm between these different worlds.

Some of those we love ardently, may go.

For those of us left behind, this is painful stuff. We are scraped up and bruised and wishing that someone would kiss it and make it better. But, there's no one who can do that work for us. We must own and navigate our own transformation, starting where we are.

In our grief, in our mourning for what was, we may not feel strong enough to do this spiritual work. However, for our planet (and our lives) to have a chance to green up and bud again, we must prune and clean and harvest and let go of what was.

We must sleep, dream, and plan.

We must savor the darkness of our messy nest.

Spring—with its cherry blossoms and birdsong and fertile sense of promise—is still a distant dream. We're slumbering in ashes, in muck, in the underbelly of life. This is powerful dream work.

Let's get to it.

The World Behind the World was originally published in *The Wonderland Files* on November 9, 2013.

Demeter

Jaclyn Piudik

Into diaphanous robes drenched
with tears wailed at the lost child,
I pour myself, my wealth
of body. Taken from me, child
of this body, child,
to darkness, flaming pits
the queen of frailty.
Black layers over her tiny frame
a woman now, she gives herself

to him who stole her
youth, innocence, feeding her
pomegranate seeds; their juice
trembles from the sides of her mouth,
streaks her chin, her neck red.
He licks, bites into her
as if she were his; and she giggles

when he washes her
clean of the ashes they sleep in.
She awakens from her dreams more beautiful
than before in the chamber of night where she rests,
greeting the newly dead.

I roam the punishing land, lost
without her, feel nothing but naked
fields, grainless, gainless, parched
heavy beneath my soles.

No temple can repay a frenzy
of ebony bed-sheets, ravenous god.

Kali

Taya Malakian

I am the one in the mask,
in the dark.
My feet buried deep in the earth
my hands covered in the grit.
I am the one who has no fear
of the blood, sweat, tears
of this world
for I am painted with them all.
I take all your suffering in with each breath
and I transmute it back into the light
that it is.
I see only truth
so your lies,
your fears,
your insecurities
mean nothing to me.
I am the one who penetrates
through your dreams of chaos
to show you what you will not see.
I am the one who ignites
the fire within you that burns
away illusion
and guides you through the night.
That deep howl inside of you
that wants to sing your truth
is the language that I speak in.
And the vast silence of the infinite
is the space in which I hear.

Lilith

Rhea Ruth Aitken

With raven hair
That flashes bright as fire
When in defiance she turns her head,
Reflecting shining and bright
In her coal dark eyes
That scan the dark moon
And the myths of night.
Red lips stained from promised fruit
That no kiss, no words
Nor deed of man can sway
To utter anything but her truth.
And glowing sleek and black
The feathered wings that dress her back
Open magnificent and strong
In dark beauty taking her flight
When all about her is so wrong.
No subordination does she stand
She owns her freedom
Shows her power
For all brave women fly on her wings.
And from her sacred lips
Words of the world's sisters sing
The mysteries of the feminine
Never again to veil her light
From dictates of mortal or immortal men.

Morning Brew

Tosha Silver

Someone told me she
leads goddess rituals
and said,
we write our dreams
draw our desires
we dance
in a circle
and throw rose petals
everything we
want always
comes true
Ooh, I said
my wish came true
too
MahaKali scared
the daylights
out of me
She drowned
me in a nearby
river
then chopped me
up and steeped
me
in Her
favorite morning
brew
She said
it tastes
gooood

Threshold

Susan Laura Earhart

Dark Creatrix breathes fire into my veins.
Rushes my senses into stampeding twilight
And rakes my flesh raw with the collision.
Bifurcates my madness so the forked tongue
Of my lie hisses into Truth.
You, demoness of my soul,
You dangle the gatekeeper's key.
Unlock pandemonium, let sweet abandon
Writhe and shake, disassembling completely
This facade created by the false gods.
Replace my mask so skilfully that neither concealment
Nor revelation triumphs.
Cast a creature in your own image
Black, sharp, biting, wild-eyed and free.

Stepping into the Light:
Heeding Bloduewedd's Call
Robin R. Corak

I recall vividly one of the first times I encountered her. I was in a small temple illuminated by just the barest sliver of a moon. There, in the darkness before me, was a woman with amber eyes and the face of an owl. I knew without a doubt that I was looking into the eyes of the goddess Bloduewedd.

I felt exhilarated.

I felt moved to tears.

I felt sick.

Literally, I felt sick. I experienced a sudden rush of energy so strong that it caused me to feel nauseous and dizzy.

Bloudewedd had made herself known and make no mistake... she was there to kick my ass into gear.

Given her frequent portrayal in The Mabinogion as a young, (initially) submissive creature, one wouldn't think of Bloudewedd as being intimidating. But while her energy was loving and light, she made it very clear that she meant business.

The timing was perfect. I had ended my marriage the previous year. Doing so had been heartbreaking, and ran counter to every instinct I had as a life-long peacemaker who dreaded rocking the boat. Shortly thereafter, I unexpectedly fell head over heels in love with another man much to the chagrin of some who felt he was too old for me and/or that I was moving on too quickly. My son was diagnosed as having special needs and I was the only parent to advocate for him. I was finding that my position at work increasingly required me to speak up, share my ideas, and be a voice for those in need.

Having previously been scared of the dark, you would think that I would have gravitated strongly towards a goddess that was "lighter." Yet, as much as I was excited to be working with Bloudewedd, I was also terrified. I was pretty comfortable with the introspection present in darkness. In addition, I had experienced paralyzing shyness as a child. Having to speak my truth was far scarier than doing the reflective internal work. Say what I *really* feel? Out loud?! Uh, no thanks. I'll just be over here in the corner talking to my shadow self...

Despite my trepidation, I was beginning to recognize the gifts granted to me by simply daring to claim my own happiness. I decided to take a huge leap of faith into Bloduewedd's arms. I began to increasingly speak my truth. My confidence surged and my accomplishments grew. I listened to my heart and I was happy.

At some point later on, I realized that my connection to Bloduewedd had faded. I could not figure out how this could have occurred with a goddess that I had once had such a fruitful relationship with. It finally dawned on me that I had again slipped back into the comfortable hibernation the darkness offered. The watery realms of emotions and the unconscious had long felt like home.

Bloduewedd's realm of rebirth and emergence? That was another story. After all, babies typically don't come into this world with a serene smile on their face and an inner knowing that it's all going to be alright. No, they come into this world kicking and screaming because they are terrified of losing the comfort and safety of the womb. Reconnecting with Bloduewedd required me to have to actually *do* something, not just think about doing it. If I were to fail, I would fail in the harsh light where everyone could see.

I didn't know what she wanted from me at first. I now realize there is still much work to be done. There are times when old childhood triggers cause me to leave things unsaid, or to not dare as greatly as I want to. At times, I feel tempted to run back to my comfort zone. Lately, I've heard her whispering in my ear, a little louder each time. She says it's time for me to be bold and to take things to the next level. She reminds me that you can fight for what you believe with love and without compromising your principles.

She has inspired me to make my voice heard, whether it is in my work, as my son's advocate, or in exploring my own creative expression. When I hesitate because speaking my truth could cause controversy, Bloduewedd grins and says that rocking the boat may be exactly what I should strive for. When I worry that I am being too vulnerable and fear encompasses me like a stifling fog, she says to me, "Screw your fear. Your voice is needed. To be of service and to fully love, you must be brave enough to be vulnerable."

I will never be the "in your face" type of bold: that's simply not who I am. I am not the storm you see coming, I am more like the river that—with great persistence and patience—has the power to transform the rock with my words and my actions. When doubt creeps in and my inner child feels compelled to quietly blend into the shadows, Bloduewedd makes herself known.

"Isn't it time you stopped worrying so much about what others might think and start worrying more about the unsung songs still left in your heart?"

Her words give me wisdom and wings, and I find the strength to let my songs pierce the darkness so that I may fly again with the grace of an owl.

Deep Breath

J. Ellen Cooper

the healer comes.
the sign proclaimed: Common Medicinal Herbs
so the plantress has a name
well, what magic do these furred periwinkle trumpets?
is it their season?
and when will the mallow seeds ripe for harvest?
Pele, i've caught the scent

i feel out along the web, a synergy of crystal raindrops on knots
of net and thread
the realization flips a switch the size of the universe.
each teacher looks up from her pruning,
the sound of static. their ears pitch and the urge to yawn.
a message travels in coloured numbers
it smells of a rich soil under nitrogenous leaves
and feels of the start of September

Pele, the tide pushes back.
a green dance has begun moonward,
the paintbrush will love this.
i can taste the herbs, chop grate grind them
drink pick breathe them

i will ink a spell that braids purpose with plant
i will prescribe the poem with a tea
and women's voices will whisper back the magic into being

they will heal from kissing leaf to finger tip and other steps
of ritual, from start to 'so mote it be.' clits will ring with it,
the women will penetrate, a vine up trunken spines,
the planet, Her surface will glow from the light
of all of those umbilical chords humming delightedly back to life

Diana the Huntress

Audrey Haney

On the isle of Delos be born a child
for like her twin brother she be wild
for beasts and birds with tooth and claw
for hounds that bite and, snarl and gnaw
her wrath is ruthless but never depraved
her emotions are honest and never enslaved
Diana her name, meaning heaven divine
the moonlight her home. The bow is her sign
she runs in wild places with hounds by the side
The hunting of stag, she always takes pride
Her moon rules emotions of all womenfolk
her love is the country, her tree is the oak
She was always a maiden, a virgin for life
for men always caused her such hatred and strife
Protector of women, the young and the crone
Defender of children away and at home
she whispers to mothers to keep a firm hand
for children need safety in this fearful land

The Soul Cries of an Irish Goddess of Darkness: The Banshee!

Yvonne Brewer

I remember the childhood image I held of her in my mind: a fragile figure with bony fingers and long silver hair. She walked slowly and fearlessly resting now and then on her wooden staff while she watched the birds in the trees or smiled at the fairies when they danced and sang her songs or listened to hear if the voices were shouting nasty words at her again. She had a shawl, sometimes it was black and sometimes it was grey. And in her pockets she always had hair combs that she combed her long hair with as she cried but I was warned to never ever pick up a comb if I found one under my bedroom window or by the bushes or under the trees. And she always had small stones in her pockets too, the ones that jump out at you because of their brightness or shape or softness and just have to be picked up. And though my Grandmother insisted that this woman was to be feared and that she screeched in the darkness of night to warn families of death, I never sensed that type of fearful energy from her.

Something intuitively told me in my childhood that the Banshee was a woman who had been powerful and pushed out of society as an outcast. The stories my Grandmother told me excited me and did not make me fearful. Even when my Grandmother used a story about the Banshee to try and make my brothers and I go to sleep one night after midnight, and knocked on my bedroom window as she howled and pretended she was the frightening wild woman herself, it did not drive any fear into me, (and unfortunately also did not work as a method to make us sleep!) Instead, I felt her presence even stronger as I saw her smiling and laughing at the nonsense she constantly had to put with from those ignorant of her greatness or fearful of it.

Growing up in an Irish Catholic culture I do not ever remember hearing the term "Goddess," I only heard about a "God." Of course, there was the Blessed Virgin Mother Mary who was looked up to and adored as our Divine Mother but the words "Mother" and "Goddess" were never placed together in the vocabulary that was preached to me. I certainly did not feel the sense of a Goddess who "ruled" or who had power in the same way that "God" or male "Saints" seemed to be given.

The curious child within—the one who hungered for answers, the one who sought to adore and accept imperfections rather than the perfect statues of a lady who was full of grace, that I respected but did not relate to—drew me to a female myth in Irish society who was frowned upon. She drew me to one who was feared and certainly not given the status of a ruler or Goddess—the Banshee, An Bean Sídhe (fairy woman).

Amidst all the frightening stories I listened to I began to understand that women who were powerful spiritually were not easily accepted in Irish society. I learned that women who chose a path that was seen as "different" were regarded as "strange." I sensed that this strangeness could be laughed at, ridiculed or ignored in order to preserve the status quo in a largely Catholic dominated society. This "difference" became associated with women who chose not to have children, women who chose to not get married, women who chose another woman as their lover, women who had children outside of marriage, women who wanted to be educated or have careers. I sensed that within Irish society and amidst all the ideas that Ireland is a warm, friendly place to be that in fact there was an element of dragging people down, a begrudgery and in my experiences of growing up in the 1970s/1980s, it was directed mainly towards women. So as a child who was very sensitive to picking up the attitudes and underlying vibes around me I quickly came to understand that the myths of the Banshee were probably created to find a space to push all the dark feminine energy that stood for difference, uniqueness, magic, power, creativity, paganism, into one character, that of a fairy woman, Bean Sídhe, (fairy woman) who was to be feared and whose cries were not to be listened to.

As I grew up and continued to have an interest and fascination in myths, fairies, spirituality I also learned that there are deep secrets and whispers and untold stories buried in the spirit of our land and I believe that the Banshee holds all those things and carries this darkness for us.

She cries the cries of our ancestors, she warns of the dangers of suppressing our wounds and burying our restless souls without sending them the love and light they so deserve and need. Ears are closed to her cries, eyes see danger and not power and tongues speak badly of her to frighten their children from wakening in the night to listen to her truths. Women fear her as their children might understand her cries or worse still their husbands might be drawn to the crying woman and reach out to her and feel sucked in by her magical charisma and power.

She is a Goddess of all that is Dark, the woman of magic and wisdom that a patriarchal and Christian society wishes to be dead. But she will not die. They killed her spirit, they buried her body and yet they cannot understand why they still hear her cry. It is her soul cries that cannot be silenced. Nothing can silence the soul.

The Banshee invites us to welcome and befriend the darkness. She holds out her hand to guide us on a journey that lets us feel the wind blowing in our hair as we comb it, to embrace death of the old ways and welcome the newness of new experiences and having walked barefoot on hills and sand that our ancestors fought for. She wants us to pick up twigs and stones and thank them for their part in helping the truth to unfold. She longs for us to see again the fairies and the magic that is around us and within the land we walk on daily. They are her people, she is their Queen and because we have lost sight of who she is, we have lost sight of her people and lost sight of our souls' journey. Our souls do not know where to go anymore, they have not been fed enough or drank enough of the juices that are dripping from the trees and grass and our ears have not heard the birds' soul songs.

She invites us back to our source, our Spirit, our Soul sisters and brothers who have gone before us.

She comes to us when we write, sing, dance, play, walk in the woods and open our hearts amongst the trees. She welcomes us home every time we refuse to close our ears and eyes to the doubting voices in our heads, when we say no to our fears, when we say yes to our inner voices and stand strong in our beliefs even though there are times we do not even understand or know where it comes from.

Inviting her into our hearts we realize that she is a maternal figure, a ruler of the soul, a nurturer of all that has been left in darkness and cries to be touched by the light. Dropping all fears and negative images about her allows us to be open to releasing a huge part of the soul wounds of Ireland's past and in this way allowing much yearned for healing, harmony and peace to unfold on every level.

Embodying Gaia

Amanda Dobby

She embodies Gaia in her every sway, prayer and step;
she has a dark side it's best not to provoke, poke or tempt.

Nothing delights her spirit more than the warm sun gently
kissing her skin;
his touch leaves a delightful afterglow she's not afraid to show.

Her heart drinks in the rain without shame or blame;
like the trees, the sky is her only aim.

Like the butterfly she flies;
she knows freedom truly arrives on the other side of the cocoon,
crumbling and demise.

Dreams are built stick by stick, like the beaver builds his dam;
everything is meticulously placed as per the grand plan.

The moon guides her like it hypnotizes and controls the rise and
fall of the tides;
her soul thrives off the flow of the ride.

Like the wind, she can blow you over if you ignore her polite
request to step aside;
she knows her direction is always hers to decide.

Serving Gaia and the Great Mother Team

Mare Cromwell

My foremost goddess appears to me as a turtle—a live one. She may be as tiny as a large coin or more than two feet across. The large turtles are always intimidating snapping turtles. Often I rescue them and have become skilled at handling the dangerous turtles so my hands stay intact.

Most Native American cultures see the turtle as Gaia. Numerous native stories tell of the world sitting on top of a turtle's back. When turtles show up auspiciously to those who are spiritually connected to Gaia, it is a potent sign that she is honoring you directly for your love for her.

I have studied with Native American teachers for more than twenty-one years. Some might call me a mystic and healer. My connection with Gaia goes deep. It shifted even more deeply when her consciousness was brought into my spirit body through a ceremony with a Native elder in June 2012. I had just been diagnosed with lymphoma and Mother started speaking to me directly after that ceremony. She offered to heal me from the cancer completely away from the doctors if I surrendered to her to the depths she would ask.

Gaia has been keeping me rather busy, to put it mildly. I am also now healed.

Truthfully, Gaia is only part of my Goddess community. In the process of writing *The Great Mother Bible,* I reconnected with the Virgin Mary, the goddess with whom I grew up. My father sent me a Miraculous Medal that winter and, to my surprise, I was told by Gaia to put it on. Instantly a powerful wash of Divine Feminine energy came over me. It stunned me. The Virgin Mary is absolutely huge spiritually and so much more than any of us young Catholic children were taught.

In 2011, Kuan Yin came forth via a gifted pipe carrier after the Divine Mother told him that she liked me and that I could become a priestess of hers. He then gave me a small statue of Kuan Yin at the request of the Mother. In the moment, I was honored and humbled but confused about how I could ever be a priestess.

This winter (2017) all twenty-one Taras arrived en masse early one morning and informed me, they were going to download their wisdom and spiritual medicine into me. I had been invoking them in ceremony for months and I suppose they determined it was time I got to know them better.

The list goes on. I call them the "Great Mother Team." More recently, Athena came in for a client of mine. I'm not sure what might happen tomorrow and whether another goddess might show up on the spiritual planes to ask me to work with her sacred energies.

The irony is that I am in my late fifties and only *now* starting to fully embrace that *I am a goddess* and my body is a sacred temple embodying the Divine Feminine (and also the Divine Masculine). I am a spiritual being who seeks to be in balance in this feminine goddess body as a fully actualized person.

Just two nights ago, a quite evolved thirty-five year old man who has been doing ceremony with me for months gifted me on my fifty-eighth birthday with a photograph of the Virgin Mary from a Bolivian Catholic chapel. Then he stayed for the night and massaged and held me and in the morning we giggled in bed. This divine young man helped wake up my essential goddess self as no man ever had (in this lifetime). We may never giggle in bed again and that is fine. His treating me like a goddess was more than I knew to ask for.

As I write this, I feel ancient Divine Feminine energies rippling through me that have been repressed all of my life. Repressing them was part of the source of my illness. They are now flowing and I'm walking differently, more poised and grounded as I claim my inner goddess. I now understand far more what it means to be a priestess.

We are all Goddesses! Yet we are not meant to be living off in a temple secluded from the hustle of everyday life. We are walking temples weaving the Mother's energies throughout our homes, workplaces, PTA meetings, and perhaps even in our churches helping to wake up the dormant Divine Feminine all around us.

Mother Gaia has a 'funny' way of continuing to remind me of her prominence in my life as 'foremost Goddess' (honestly though, she seems to be so much more than a 'goddess' to me). Several times now while en route to visit a sacred site devoted to another emanation of the Divine Feminine, she plops a live turtle in the middle of the road for me to rescue. She's rather clever and the turtle is quite aware it is being sent as a messenger.

I carry the turtle to safe haven off the road and thank Mother for the reminder to stay true to my soul contract to serve her and help far more people wake up to her sacred presence and Quantum Divine Love as our Planetary Caretaker. She knows I get easily distracted.

There is a beautiful New World coming in presently and the 'Great Mother Team' needs all of us to wake up and step up. It is time!

Gaia: Our Earth

Rhea Ruth Aitken

Beneath your feet, I breathe for you.
Deep within me,
Fuelled by burning rocks and ancient fires
I live so you may live upon me.
The waters of my soul flow to sustain you,
All that seeds within my body
All that grows from my skin
Are my gifts to you.
When you stop to touch the Earth
Do you feel the quiver of my pleasure?
Or feel my heartbeat rising with your own?
When you lie upon me,
Abandon yourself to my embrace
Do you feel the oneness of soul on soul?
When you dance barefooted
Echoing rhythms of my own heart in your steps
Do you feel me flowing through your very being?
When you eat the medicines of my garden
Do you know they sustain and heal your body?
And when you pluck a flower or catch a leaf
Do you think of me and all I give?
I am Gaia, Earth Mother
Duchess of the forests, fields and meadows
Princess of the seas and rivers
Queen of the hills and mountains
Goddess of All.
Sing to me and I will sing you the songs of the Earth.
Dance upon me and I will take your hand
And show you the spirit of wholeness,
The ecstasy of living with freedom in your soul.
Touch me, tend me
Drink in my colors, my scents, my beauty
For I am all and everything

And in my love for you, I give it all
So you may thrive.
But I am living too
So do not forget me
Or take my gifts in vain.
For if I were to die,
If my body ceased to be
There would be no future
No beauty, no bounty, no life.
Darkness and oblivion will take me.
And you.
Care for me, respect me, honor me
Pray for me and stand up for me,
Take action for my life as I do for yours.
Rescue me from the hands of those
That have no love for me
And take without gratitude life from all of us.
I call to you from my burning heart
To be my daughters and priestesses,
To keep my living mystery.
I am Gaia. I am Mother.

The Mayan I'x

Julia W. Prentice

I'x—Goddess or
More than goddess
She is Earth Mother
Mother of all children
Earth that cares for,
Nourishes us

She is feline
Whiskered visage
Rippling power
Springing jaguar
Soft and feminine
Sinew and supple
Shaman and Grandmother
Midwife to us all

We should worship
On her stone altar
Or in her resplendent nature
On her day we should
Respect her, for
What she is for us

See calendar wheel
Spin, ancient to modern
Birthing us and the world
She rises power
Inside our blood
Inside all things
I'x — Earth-Mother
Heal us all

Healing

Paraschiva Florescu

the moon watches over me, tonight
its wholeness fills me up like a sea
still and complete. I have loved her for so long.
like a pure mother
it feeds me her white bones
touching and sucking.
her face of light
bright it blinds me.
I dance to her, crawling clinging
to the wet earth of night.

tonight: a sacrifice

or should I pray
to the small god that made me whole again.
or to her,
dressed in the pale ghosts of time
and timelessness.
she brought me home
untouched, a lover that did not break
but sewn me like a tattered doll, my lover
a white miracle.
I offer myself to her.

a sacrifice
my warm crimson blood dissolves
drops of gratitude:
pain cures pain.
there is no going back
no turning point.
a final catharsis
I dance
until branches fall and crumble at my feet
a broken tree: rootless—
I am no more.

Mother Moon, Goddess Moon

Maureen Kwiat Meshenberg

Mother Moon
Goddess Moon
darkness of the world
expanding
the sacredness of
your light moves
through the depths
between my
mundane and shattering
dying and rising I come.

Mother Moon
Goddess Moon
cradle me
womb of my soul
womb of life's breath
through the deep waters
of my birthing
strip me back to my naked soul
layers of fear that now cling
let me make peace with
my losses and my endings
of my path stepping.

Mother Moon
Goddess Moon
let the tears of my falling
sooth the seeds of life
rising
roses that bloom
and color me with love
from my heart emerging
all the considerable struggles

labor pains of my understanding
my birth from my dying.

Mother Moon
Goddess Moon
she soothes my
soul's battles of life
finds my way back
to who I am
sweet transformation
contracting
the aches of my becoming
let me leave the old stories
in the embers of my past.

Mother Moon
Goddess Moon
I rise with wings
like the dragonfly
the phoenix
and the powerful eagle
spreading wide and high
I now take my flight.

Mother Moon
Goddess Moon
it is time
my howl and my cry
rise to find its moment
to be born to new life
through the celestial light
of my Mother Moon night.

The Great Lesson of the Moon Goddess

Vrinda Aguilera

Ebb and flow
Wax and wane

The rhythms of the moon queen
Each day she edges a slice more towards wholeness
Wordlessly, without complaint she paints in her sphere
With poise and grace she hovers
Her eyes opening, seeing

Her journey to fullness pushes and pulls
A force that emanates from female bodies of waters on Earth's surfaces
Echoed in the swell of waves and tides of Mother Ocean
The cycle of women's hormonal ebb and flow

Ebb and flow
Wax and wane

Until our moon goddess reaches her full ripeness
A glistening sky pearl, jewel of the heavens
The cloudy night skies that have enfolded her
Gather their shadowy drapes and part
Revealing her cooling splendor

She glistens, shines, giving audience to all below
The living sentient beings who drink in her beauty and wonder
Misty, cooling mother
We offer reverence to your splendor

Then, the momentary pause of breath half held on the inhale
The inevitable exhale descends, following on its tail
For anything alive is never stagnant
Yet swims through its own cycle of dynamic evolution
The great lesson continues

The Queen of Heaven
Nanci Bern

In the month of Elul, the Earth, our world is born. In the following month of Tishrei, we are born, specifically on Rosh Hashanah. It is said in these two months, the Divine is very close: The Goddess, The Queen of Heaven walks in the garden; the same garden that we walk in.

'Hineni' is Hebrew for 'here I am.' When we are called by Spirit we answer, 'Hineni,' 'Here I am.'

When we ask this Queen for Her name, she answers "Eh He Yeh," I am that I am.

But for these two months, I invite you to think that, She tells us "Hineni" and we tell Her "Eh He Yeh"

The Divine Presence

What is the splendour of the royal divine?
The hand that offers the beginning of time.
Who's wind of beauty's breath
fills form with its spirit?
Our hands reach toward,
a grasp tremulous,
urged by the pulse of earth
and heart of our soul.

This time, when earth has again come into its rebirth,
when the last harvest offers its cool time bounty
and we begin our own new season,
the holy is in this place and calls to us.
We walk in the garden verdant with the scent of earth's turning
and hear, "Hineni."
"Here I am."
In a swirl of spirit
vines wend themselves, with leaves green as hope,
into a path that leads to life's vibration.

"Remember," is whispered to our souls,
"I walk with you at your birth and hold you up.
I tell you I am here when you forget,
I only ask that you tell me who you are when you remember."

Like the light that makes flowers translucent in petal,
we become iridescent in tone
and answer "Eh he yeh"
"I am who I am,"
for this is all we can be.

And so we return and
step forward into our prayers that are woven
with our joy and tears,
with our questions and yearning wrapped around us.

I am a Daughter of Hera

Hayley Arrington

How do I write about my Goddess, Hera? When I realized it was Hera who had been whispering my name, I was intrigued. I decided to listen and she led me to an older pre-patriarchal Goddess: A Goddess of women, Goddess of the heavens, the Earth, and the sea. Galaxia, I whisper, and cast my eyes heavenward, for it is from her that the Milky Way spilled forth out of her benevolent breast. She is Mother, yet she encompasses all that womanhood is and can be.

She found me years before I became a mother. I believed in Goddess and felt close to many particular ones, but when Hera called to me, I knew that here was a Goddess who wanted me for her priestess; to praise her name and let other women know that Hera is there for them should they need her. Now that I have a son, I realize why Hera has for so long been a patron and a challenger to heroes. She is a woman's Goddess, but we birth sons, as well as daughters, and it has long been our sons who stray from the Goddess.

Hera challenges heroes to become their true selves. She challenges me to become my true self and to strive for all I can do. Even though it was much later in her worship that she became known as "Queen of the Gods" there is a good reason for that title. She is demanding. She is also benevolent. Hera is a native Goddess who was married off to conqueror god, Zeus. Because she was so widely loved, she became Queen and Consort to the new supreme god in charge. Because she is a Goddess of women, she can be a queen for us. For me she is regal. She is commanding. She is also kind and tender.

In my years of praising Hera, I have also grown close to two other Goddesses who are deeply connected to her. One is her daughter, Hêbe. Hêbe was born from Hera parthenogenically, without the aid of a father. Her name means youth. Hêbe may actually be a double of Hera; she essentially gave birth to herself. In myth, Hêbe is a cupbearer to the gods, and so, for me, her symbols are the water jug and chalice.

The second Goddess I praise in conjunction with Hera and Hêbe is Iris. Iris is a messenger of the gods and her name means rainbow. Visually, a rainbow connects the heavens to the sea and/or the earth, so makes for a beautiful metaphor of bringing messages to the realm of the gods. Iris is also the handmaiden to Hera. In ancient art, we find that Hêbe and Iris are often conflated. In this way, they may both be seen as daughters of Hera. In one myth, Iris goes to the river Styx and collects water from it so that the gods may take an oath by it. In this way, Iris is also a cupbearer. For me, I usually visualize Iris as winged and wearing a rainbow dress.

The Hesperides are also connected to Hera. They are a group of nymph-priestesses who tend the Garden of Golden Apples. In this garden, there is a serpent who lives peaceably there. This garden is Hera's abode. I call myself, as Hera's priestess, her Daughter, and a Hesperid, because these terms poetically describe my relationship to my Goddess.

Hera is a beautiful and complex Goddess who is calling women to hear her. I am so happy that I heard her call my name.

In Praise of Holda

Chelsea Arrington

Holda: Maiden, Mother, and Crone.
Queen of Mysteries and secrets unknown;
Hares attends you in your secret bower
As You conjure the ancient power.
In glen and forest, near lake and stream,
You spin the future as you dream.
Queen of Witches and hunt so wild
Your song beckons every child
To Your cottage in the forest so deep
Where You teach them to fly as they sleep.
For You are the witch of fairy lore
Goddess of night-time and spells galore,
Whose story was untold and perverted
In order to make the Old Ways subverted
That women's mysteries might be forgot;
That our knowledge and vision be for naught.
Yet we are Your daughters and speak Your name
Your ancient ways we hereby reclaim
That we may hear the song of the Earth
And women's mysteries will know rebirth.
Holda, we call You that we may take flight
Upon Your broomstick into the night!

My Antique Tibetan Singing Bowl

Maureen Lancaster

She is imperfect, this Grand Lady. She is wobbly looking. She is showing her age yet she sings with an inner beauty that makes her shine. Being handmade, she is full of imperfections and this is what makes her unique and individual in her sound. She reminds us that we don't have to be someone else's idea of perfect to be "perfection."

There was a clear and distinct female energy radiating from this sculpted piece of metal. I had never experienced a spirit energy emitting from a bowl before, let alone an energy with a gender. But there was no denying the fact that this bowl housed a very strong presence...

The first intuitive connection I had to the spirit presence within this very old bowl was of the energy of the Tibetan Buddhist Goddess Tara who encompasses the virtues of mercy, peace and compassion and is also known for her powers of protection. In digging deeper, I could also relate this female energy to Saraswati, the Divine Consort of Lord Brahma, the Hindu God of Creation. She is known as the Goddess of learning, knowledge and wisdom. Saraswati is all about understanding spiritual power through the use of speech, "The Word," meaning that our words create our reality.

Once I had connected with the spirit of this bowl, I found that I could not think, talk or write about her without being overwhelmed by her energy. Toe to head, an upward surge of energy would course through my body. She wanted my attention and she most definitely had it! She had a mission to accomplish and a message that needed to be told; a message to be documented. I can only relate what my human understanding allows but with the help of my spirit and earthly guides I will do my best in relating what I feel is "her" message to all of us...

First, we are to be reminded about the power of the spoken word and the fact that we have been given the ability to manifest our reality. The voice of this bowl resounds to the musical note of G, which is associated with the throat chakra, the seat of our physical voice. This is no coincidence in my mind. We are being reminded that we need to begin telling ourselves everyday that we are indeed "somebody" and in the telling we can then create our reality from a place of self-love. From that simple beginning we can then grow into our highest potential.

We need to become keenly aware of the words that we use everyday for they do indeed create our reality, our perceptions. If we constantly choose negative words to describe ourselves and our lives then we will find our world to be one that is unfulfilling, frightening and hurtful. Situations will be perceived as against us. We will attract people into our lives who will hold us back and cause us pain. If we choose, however, to see the bright side, to see our value and that of our fellow beings, then we will notice that more and more positive situations and people will arise, providing nourishment to our souls.

I believe the spirit of the bowl wishes me to tell the story of love, compassion and the importance of harmony and balance. The energies she carries with her remind us of our beginnings when we were created as equals, when we were closely connected to our spiritual roots; when we knew our purpose. We have lost track of the original values that we were given so very long ago: empowerment, unconditional love, cooperation and stewardship upon which to build our world.

In connecting with her energy, I have had words enter into my consciousness that I would not normally use, words such as apocalypse, the Greek word for "lifting of the veil" or "revelation," and illumination, words that represent the opening of our "eyes" to see clearly so that we may grow in the light of Spirit. She is letting us know that it is time to end ways of being that do not nurture our souls, that do not allow us to see the Divine in all of us.

Another female energy connected with this bowl is that of Lilith, traditionally known as the first wife of Adam, demonized because she challenged God and Adam by refusing to be subservient. Her energy has surfaced to remind us all, that without living within our own power, without living with our truths, we open ourselves up to suffering at the hands of others.

This bowl has spurred the creation of this book to not only tell my story but to spread the message of that gentle spirit within it; to tell us that we need to regain an understanding of who we are and where we have come from; to let us know that we are not alone. We are reminded of our "oneness," our interconnectedness and of the importance of compassion and love for ourselves and our fellow man.

To realize our highest potential as a people, we need to reactivate the Divine Feminine and the Divine Masculine aspects of ourselves...

Sun Goddess Amaterasu

Tammy Takahashi

If I could accompany you
Amaterasu Omikami
Great goddess of the celestial realm
Given reign over the skies above
And all the ruling gods

Sister of Moon
Sister, too, of Storms
Of rages latent and manifest,
Reflector of the world's cosmic dance,
Sublime provider of light

If I could sit with you
As you weave a calm and peaceful world
To gain true understanding
Of what we stand to lose
When you enter the cave's shadows

Where you once indignantly retreat
Turning your back to creation
Casting our world
Into a darkness so sudden and deep
That our cries, too, are smothered

Together, now, in the cave,
This close to your towering certitude,
On this side of light and dark
With you who have generated both,
I begin to weep

For you will eventually
Emerge from the cave
And the world will brighten again,

And the gods will resume their duties
Put on hold to lure you out

But I, who have sought so long,
Can fathom you no more easily
When you shine your rays upon me
Than I do in this cave
Your wild wrath having destroyed it all

This is a terrible despair
Yet slowly, achingly, life stirs again
I tilt my head toward your heavenly glow
And grasp the wisdom of the light
That teaches me how to meet you

Life giving, flowering sun goddess,
I learn: that your gift of our continuance
Is as inevitable as the descent
Into blackest depths that return us
To our illumined heart of self

Help Bring Back the Goddess from Exile

Krishna Rose

M ary Magdalene is a fascinating woman in history, yet she has sadly been misrepresented for centuries. Recently, controversy has stirred around her life as to whether or not she was the wife of Jesus, and whether or not they conceived children together. A fantastic tale is told that these children went on to allegedly become the European Kings, Queens, and Popes of the past. Yet, to me, this isn't what makes Magdalene's life so intriguing. What makes her so special is her story: the story of a beautiful woman whose life narrative became so unnecessarily tainted.

I became fascinated with Saint Mary Magdalene many years ago, not merely because she is a woman whose story has been twisted by some cruel twist of fate, but because through her we can understand our own femininity, and our subsequent struggle with the dominating male powers existent in this world today. Magdalene's struggle is familiar to us because we have all lived our own version of it. We can each tell a story of injustice, disgrace, invalidation, mistreatment, shame and silence: the story of when our own inner Goddess became exiled.

Mary Magdalene was a princess in the line of Benjamin, sister to Martha and Lazarus. She was a very wealthy woman—having inherited an entire village from her father—and became a principal leader in the early Jesus movement, funding his tours and retreats. Magdalene was an esteemed, influential teacher and renowned healer in her own right, leading masses of people for years to come after the Crucifixion. Yet, lamentably, the church decided—300 years later—to depict this powerful, spiritual woman as a "whore," in order to ruin her pure reputation as the "Apostle to the Apostles": a title Jesus himself gave her.

To me, Magdalene's misrepresentation as a "whore" is especially disheartening, as it sadly served to protect and preserve a dogmatic, male-focused view of God, to the complete exclusion of the Goddess. So what happened? Why had the mere idea of associating a woman with Goddess become heretical, leaving those who represented the Goddess to be viewed as worthy of a good hanging or burning?

Rather than exploring the ugly trail of lust for power, avarice and ignorance left behind by the rulers of the Middle Ages, I invite you to shift your focus to an inspiring prophecy instead. It is predicted in the ancient Jewish scripture of Micah, that by returning Magdalene to the side of her husband, Jesus, all the imbalances in the world today shall be healed. What could be more exciting! Here is what it says:

As for you, O Magda-Eder (Watchtower over the Flock, Magdalene), you cry aloud, for you have no King at your side, your former dominion will be restored to you, for you were forced out of the City, and have camped in the open fields for too long. You have withered in agony, and almost perished at the hands of your councilors! Oh great magnificent Tower (Magdal), Kinship will come to you, the daughter of Jerusalem.

Because of Magdalene's own banishment, and the agony she suffered, we women of the world have also withered over the ages, and learned not to shine. We have—to one degree or another— disconnected ourselves from our own creativity, from the healing gifts of nature, from The Goddess herself and, ultimately, from ourselves. This has been our only survival mechanism, and it saved us from being hung and burned at the stake. Yet, because of this oppressive history, to this day our DNA reels in this under-handed belief that all women are "Evil Eve's" and "Whores": this is the message that we have all felt running through the subconscious veins of our modern culture. It's now time to let those veins bleed out, for the Goddess is fulfilling her prophecy and returning from exile!

As I meditate on the story of Mary Magdalene and touch upon these powerful core issues, I can deeply relate to her being publicly defamed like this for centuries, and feel myself housing a portion of her shame within my own psyche. To call any woman a whore is a terrible disgrace! And even though the Catholic Church has issued a formal apology for having cast Magdalene as a repentant prostitute, the restoration of her dignity and sanctity has just begun.

This is where each of us comes in. I challenge all of us women to shine the light on the Goddess. We can begin by recognizing her light in each of us. Let us rewrite the story of the exiled Goddess by writing new chapters in the books of our own lives. Let go of the shame. The restoration of the Divine Feminine is a necessary part of healing the wounded psyche of men and women all over the world today. It is something I feel so passionately about—making right this wrong—in the hopes that all women, and ultimately The Goddess Herself, may be rightly situated as Divine, once again. For the whole of Divinity is incomplete without the Goddess. God and Goddess—the Divine Masculine and Divine Feminine potencies— must reign *together* for the world to truly thrive again. We cannot dismiss either one.

The Arthurian legends of the Holy Grail believed that the restoration of the Bride of Christ, the wife of Jesus, would heal the wasteland and cause the deserts to bloom once more. I pray to see this prophecy come true in our lifetime, for indeed, the deserts of our hearts are in need of water.

The Song of the Rose

Frances Roberts-Reilly

Before the darkness of our wounding,
falling from consciousness
we forgot the spiraling
super-nova fiery rose
of our begetting.

I appeared. Miraculously it seemed. Painted on a cloak
of the Holy Virgin,
in rosy red-fire.

Meanwhile on earth
I lived dark and dangerous
in flesh, blinded with paranoia.
Touching the wound
ached with the perfume of sorrow.
petals on the Cross, crucified.

Escaping only when the cultural mirrors
of our collective narcissism were smashed.
With feral courage some saw the terror of their own betrayal
were themselves
broken too.

The great fire collecting in caves,
deserts, on mountaintops, icecaps—
rose up.
The passionate song from beyond is heard
singing through earth, through air, through water.

The enfolded super nova rose
is the ensouled rose now resurrected:
The heart-rose.
The compass.
The rose-fire blossoming with direction.

The Boat Coming In

Fateme Banishoeib

Vesta the goddess of heart focus and haven
This is the trilogy I want to live
All my life packed in boxes again
By rude hands not knowing the value of fragrances
I travel in time
Wish of growing roots of security and serenity
The Whisper tells me to sense
I rushed fast forward a life for six
Trying to please the mission
Pleasing I found conflict
The conflict between the good girl and the multitudes
An eternal state of confusion
Masked by fortune and fame
I embraced globetrotterness
I created boxes travelling the world
No fun anymore
In the dark confusion I can't see
The Whisper says to open the door
I don't see it
My *senses can smell it and feel it*
So I create a story to find the door to get home
The journey of remembering who I am

Venus and Scout

Gerry Ellen

A beautiful morning begins: I walk out onto the small redwood deck so close to the earth, sensing the sky turning from foggy grey to cobalt blue. I hear the hummingbirds frantically flying to feed newly hatched babies from jellybean-sized eggs to wispy spear-beaked younglings. The winds pick up, and the most radiant sunrise takes over the atmosphere.

I am part of nature and she is an abundant part of me. I have a head full of dreams from sleep the night before. I write them down. I research them for alignment, flow and metaphors. I gaze out into the sanctuary of succulents and flora. I feel grateful.

I've developed a routine over time (practice makes perfect, right?) that involves everything from self-love and care to writing in my journal while tea is brewing, to lying in supine position on the floor with a chosen crystal or gemstone resting on a chakra in need.

Something stirs inside of me, though. It's indefinable on most days, yet tugs undeniably at my heart. I listen closely, for these are distinct feelings and yearnings propelling me into action of a different kind, a fresher kind. I've been spending some time on the central coast of California, craving solitude and connection as two sides of the same coin. It is exactly the balm I need. Any residual join inflammation has become a non-issue; the Mediterranean climate agrees with every part of my body.

It is Venus, the goddess immanent and surrounding me, coursing through me.

Oh Venus retrograde, my personal goddess of the cosmos, who is so kind to me. She grips me ever so strongly with her lust for love and money as she shows me her sensitivities that persuade me to let go and allow the natural rhythm of her magic to take hold. I feel her most in the early evenings, when she rises as the brightest light after the sun has set.

I bow to her, as the memories of days of yore come flooding in. That's her job though, to propel healing, to cause a do-over if needed, to review, to do everything under her power to "re" all that we are and all that we hold dear. It may not always be pleasant or welcomed, but I revere her. Not a single human has ever visited her surface. She's too elusive and far away to allow that. She only illuminates our consciousness for purposes of the here and now. She is my goddess of all things nature and freedom, and I look for her radiance every night.

I stare and gaze in awe. I talk to her. I'm inspired by her. She is everywhere, living inside all of us, yet I have a special bond with her. She offers me the chance to take my time; she doesn't allow me to go where my best self is of little use, and she certainly shines and dims each day for others to take notice of her, too.

In fact, Venus went into hiding for six weeks just Scout, my best friend and muse, and I left for our coastal trip. I can honestly say that it felt planned that way, as I always enjoy delving deeper and discovering the ins and outs of my psyche. This was now a time to settle into a love on the earthly plane, to notice that everything I see, smell, hear, taste and touch becomes a part of me through the filter of imprints made upon the fabric of my essence by our pawed predecessors. As we settled into our new coastal life, the synchronous union of body, mind and spirit became all wrapped up in the cells of my lungs, heart and soul, willing and able to spread it to humanity on a moment's notice.

When I'm deep into nature I am free; nothing else matters at such times. Serendipity and simplicity are my friends, and they alone can transform an entire moment into a miracle of sorts, just as when Venus worked her magic to bring Scout, my best friend and muse, into my life two years ago.

After being abandoned and subsequently rescued, he has blossomed like a soft rose. The union we share delivers and inspires an awareness of happiness and sincerity we share with whoever crosses our path. This is what our purpose is, and has become. We hold nothing back. We are here to rise, and be, to morph and experience all this intricate globe of ours has to offer. It's a daily practice, and one in which no two days are alike. Some are messy and challenging, while others are extraordinary and unexpected. Some don't seem to fit at all, whilst others resonate as if predetermined by something greater than our selves. Past years and previous downfalls have been replaced with hope, prayer, peace, love and a faith that all is well.

Our divine connection has been the greatest blessing of my life. He's a teacher, an independent spirit, a puppy at heart and an intelligent rat terrier mix who has captured my soul. We spend countless hours each day adventuring, carousing and sharing who we are with others. Scout even recently narrated his own story; I was merely holding the pen. He has a language of gestures that continually astonish me in a golden way. His velvet ears, his lithe and muscular body, and his learning skills: they speak to a feeling of utter gratitude that migrates from his furry body to my gracefully aging one. I've promised him the world. He returns it to me, twofold.

Oh Venus! I stand under the starry heavens and breathe her in. I'm captivated by her essence, especially when she's so close to a crescent moon or that enormous planet, Jupiter. She can dance with the best of them, Mars included. She is feminine perfection, the emanation that brings my heart into its fullness, the light when I feel dark, and the goddess that whispers glory into my senses. I treasure her wildness and her natural propensity to shift energy and make things happen, as they are now. Even when she's in hiding, her spirit is felt through revelations and reflections.

My only words to her are: "Ah Venus, there you are. I love you, and I thank you." Venus responds with reminders of love, and brings me back to myself. I feel this core, and through the goddess's power, Scout does the same.

Aletheia

Paraschiva Florescu

one two three
leaves
falling off my body
like trees like trees
I change
I falter.

I dance with the dead
what a delight
their shadows on the blank walls of my mind
enchant me
untouchable as yesterday.

I dance sunsets
as red skies melt and linger on my arms
like hot blood
and charms.

seven seas heaving inside
they carve my body into something new
a metamorphosis that gets me through
day by day.

each heartbeat:
a mantra of life
I am I am I am
throbbing and pulsing
red cells that harm.

one two three
it goes on and on—a fault
like everything else.

do not be fooled by the
papery feel of my heart or my dull
words that speak nothing of love
of art.

do not be fooled by my weakly disguise
from the dark ashes I rise
like a broken white moon of bone
I am
never defeated.

Aphrodite

Alison Stone

Skimmed like cream from the sea, I came
with curves and symmetry, with birdsong
laughter, jeweled combs in my nacre hair.
Came with gifts of zing, jolt, dazzle, thrill.

Not endurance—time's quotidian grind,
marriage's cold noose
around the finger. Not fidelity,
that dour maiden aunt.

I give love in its unfettered
glory—*wow, yes*, gratitude
of captivated hearts, of bodies'
truest hungers felt, and filled.

Life continues.
Work, wars, vendors'
sing-song at the marketplace.
Olives ripen on familiar trees.

Yet each surface of this known
world sparkles with a patina of gold,
beauty that has always shone, unnoticed.
Now, your eyes are open
and you see.

The Green Mantle of Brigid

Thea Prothero

I first became aware of Brigid—in the form of St. Brigid—because my Gran, who was an Irish traveler, used to regularly pray to her. My Gran was beholden to no one, fearless, but at the same time, stoic and stubborn. I remember her clinging to the small silvery St. Brigid medal—part of her Rosary—when the rain hammered on the wooden roof and all the buckets inside were full, asking for relief or shelter. She made Brigid crosses from hay and dried grass when she sat on her stool in the balmy summer evenings, a roll-up (cigarette) in her mouth, a huge tea pot at her side, blessing each one with unknown exotic (to me) words, before continuing to the next, and the next. Brigid gave her comfort and guidance—Gran would swear this, even when her rheumatism made her unable to walk or use her hands. Her faith was absolute.

These memories of my Gran are cherished and remain absolutely clear, even though she passed away over 35 years ago. But saints and what I believed they represented, were something I felt little personal connection with. However as I spent time in my childhood living in the wilds and wild places, I have always experienced a strong sense of belonging to the forests and moors. I remember subliminally being aware of the spirit of woods and rivers as a child. I could sense the surging life force of spring and the silent heartbeat of winter. The bond this formed was profound and inherent and I believe to this day, that we are one.

When my daughter was 6 or 7, I started following the Druidic path that had always been my destiny to do. One day, shortly after beginning Druidic training, I attended a workshop on Celtic Goddesses. Although it was a brief overview, my intention was to use it as a starting point, if you will, to future study and contemplation. It was here, I had an epiphany as I journeyed with Brigid in meditation. I suddenly knew that she had always been with me and was a protector of my daughter. I was immensely comforted, as though wrapped in swaddling cloths like a baby. Her healing love radiated through me like sunshine on new green leaves as they awaken.

I wanted to shout from the highest mountain, I felt like Gwion Bach when he first tasted the three drops from the Cauldron of inspiration and became Taliesin—I was completely alive for the first time!

From then on, the Goddess has been with me as my constant companion. I see and feel Her presence in every aspect of my life: from my daughter's infectious laughter, to each blade of grass under foot. I see Her in the glorious summer swelling of courgettes and apples in autumn and feel the gentle blossom filled breezes of spring. I rest with Her in the snow-covered death of winter, waiting to be re-born again every year. Our favorite ritual is Imbolc, and we begin preparations during the previous autumn by planting 20 snowdrops each year, (19 for each flame-keeper and one for the Goddess who attends the sacred flame on the 20th day), as the ritual approaches we make Brideogs from the cut branches of our apple tree and cloth in shades of green to please the Goddess. On the eve of Imbolc we place the Brideog in her bed by the fireplace, and chant songs of devotion and praise. A piece of cloth is hung outside in the hope that the Goddess will bless it as she walks by, and the mantle is used in healing and comport for the following year. I consult Her most nights through prayer, and give thanks for the blessings She has bestowed during each day. Her counsel is wise and honest and I often look at situations or issues anew— with fresh eyes, after meditating or asking for guidance.

Last year, I was working particularly deeply with my ancestors —my beloved Gran was constantly with me, guiding me to visit places in search of precious connections. My search lead me to Ireland— known as Her green mantle—where Brigid whispers in the rural greenness, and kindness of strangers had Brigid's name imprinted throughout the land. I was guided to Kildare the birthplace of St Brigid, where there is a wonderful merging of pagan and Christian beliefs. I was permitted to light two candles from the perpetual flame, kept by the welcoming nuns at Solas Bhride—one for my Gran to carry back to my family, and one to enable me to work more deeply with the fire aspect of the Goddess. I sat with two of the generous and open-hearted nuns and had a much appreciated discussion over steaming hot tea, about the Goddess, the saint and my old Gran. Before I left, I underwent an overwhelming desire to present the centre with my Gran's tiny nickel St Brigid medal. I hesitated because it is one of the only treasured commemorations I have of Gran. However, I instinctively knew that both Gran and the Goddess wanted me to do this.

Looking back at this visit, I now understand how the deep intrinsic love of Brigid has always been part of my ancestral DNA —through my Gran, and probably generations her mother's before, continuing through myself and to my daughter. Now there is part of me in Kildare, connected to my ancestral mother-line through my Gran, and Beloved Brigid, saint and Goddess, as it's always been and will be, forever.

Diana, the Huntress

Alise Versella

The horned woman resides in the forest beside the bark king

But the pelted beasts run not as fast as she

The feathered ones get lost in the expanse of her wings
The river ripples under the quake of her feet
The wind sighs through the grass

And night crawlers bask
      in her looming shadow
Hunters cannot tame her arrows
She is the mounted skull you'll never possess

No, my heart you will never possess
      never will you reach close enough to pierce this flesh

She pledges loyalty only to the earth
The girl is queen
      sovereign to herself.

The Goddess of Notre Dame

Zoe Maynard

Spectators look on at the
facades and aesthetics, I feel
her presence as she wanders
through the sacred halls.

The stained glass gains her
vibrant aura from the touch of
her elegant hand, juxtaposed elegance
paralleling the realm of
artistic power that she rules.

Who is she?

Will she burn the ageing
foundation and build another?
Decadent fortunes and strange
faces.

My eye catches the dust,
and twitches.

My body rebels, her
magnetism draws me close;
her words are not plastic utterances,
they are the riches of the world,
gold and silver lines on the forsaken
grounds of Notre Dame.

Crimson settles on her pale
face, untouched from the sins,
the dark temptations of the new
generation.

The mirror stares through
my glazed eyes, and I realize
that I am the goddess that I wish to be.

Circus Princess Soaring

Chameli Ardagh

Who could guess that the doorway into Durga's power
would be through such a radical vulnerability?
That you will have to lay down that sword in order to
pick up Her demon-slaying dagger made of pure awareness.
That only when you relax your grip on control,
She will hand you her Cosmic Frisbee of Light
which catapults your longing into
the heart of creation itself.

Who could guess that the demons will rarely
show up with Dracula teeth and wart-covered noses?
That their disguise is so much more clever than that,
as they wrap themselves around you like a second skin,
panting their familiar complaints and self-justifications
into your ear until you believe that this is all there is to it all.

Who could guess that all that fixing and fighting,
resisting and improving yourself would
keep you an eternal arm's length away from the real medicine?
And that you, in those moments you remember love,
are soaked.

Who would guess that another name for
Durga's tiger is Paradox?
That once you are up on its back,
with this big hot furry animal between your legs,
the content of that heavy backpack
of theories and reasons of yours
will drop down to the ground as an offering of mulch.
And that the beat of the tiger's heart will remind you,
everything that happens is the path,
is the practice,
is the process.

Who could ever guess that underneath that
undercover identity of yours
there is a circus princess soaring with
divine bravery and devotion?
Her holy body made of crazy longing and the kindest light.
And that the fire of love,
sometimes concentrated and dangerously ruthless,
other times a vast and calm underlying pulse,
is your very being,
and it is here She pulls you real close.

Ode to Durga

Jhilmil Breckenridge

Your face reflects the light of Shiva
Your ten arms come from Vishnu
Your feet from Brahma
Your long tresses from Yama's light
Your breasts formed from Somnath, the Moon God
Your waist from Indra, the King of Gods
Your legs and thighs from Varuna's light
Your toes from the light of Surya
Your fingers come from the light of the Vasus, Ganga's children
Your nose from Kuber
Your teeth from the light of Prajapati
Your eyes have the light of Agni
Your eyebrows from the Sandhyas—sunrise and sunset
Your ears from the light of Vayu

Every cell in your body divine,
You are Shakti and you are power absolute
You are the Mother, eternally benevolent
Some call you Durga, though you have many forms
Nine the number of spiritual significance
Nava—for new—also nine in Hindi
Nava-ratri, Nava-patrika, Nava-graha,
Nava-Durga

As Shailaputri, you are the daughter of the mountains
As Brahmacharini, you practice devout austerity
As Chandraghanta, you are worshipped for peace and prosperity
As Kushmanda, you are the Creator of the Universe
In Skanda Mata, you are the Mother of Lord Kartikeya
Oh Katyayani, goddess daughter of Sage Kata, we worship you
on Day Six
Kaal Ratri, dark like Goddess Kali, fearless and breathing fire,
bless us

As Maha Gauri, washed clean by Shiva, you are peaceful, calm
and white
Siddhidatri, blissful and blessed with all siddhis, you are blessed
with divine healing

You are Fearless, Female, Divine, Eternal
You are Creator, Destroyer, Preserver
You are black, you are white, you are dirty, you are clean
You are Durga. You are me and I am you
You are in every woman and every woman is in you
You are. You are. You are.

Iris Supplication

Chelsea Arrington

Iris, queen of sea and sky
The rainbow embodied
On golden wings you fly.
Give me this morning
Your unfettered grace.
Smile upon me
With your rainbowed face.

Goddess Lakshmi
Maalika-Shay Devidasi

An Opening:
A portal of Effortless and Continual Love...
Existing Inside a Galaxy of Red, Answered Prayers.
A spool of Golden thread,
Who wheels its self into Abundant Form.
Reaching Toward the heart of the Beloved...
Given by the Divine hands of Emerald Gold Energy.
She Has Arrived.
Her hair flows as new Planets form, while old comets release.
Breaking into New Births of reverent Divine Ecstasy...
She spills her Golden Pink Smile Into the Vast Horizon.
Her Lips, a pink Memory of Infinity...
Her giving Hands spill cosmic Prosperity from the Heavens.
We Open our Hungry Mouths to receive Our well Deserved Gifts.
The Sacrament of Nourishment,
Thee Attractor of Boons as Honeyed-Bliss,
Which Come in Over-Flowing amounts.
She Mounts Us on the Summit of Her plane.
She Mounts Us on Her Sovereign Beach of Dreams.
With Pink waves that undulate the Green, Sweet, Reflection
of Her Beauty.
With Waves, that undulate the Depth of Her Ever-Endearing
Direction.
Her Divine Love is a field of infinite Knowingness...
Know Her as Sri Maha Lakshmi.
See Her within your All- Auspicious smile
And Ever-Blooming, Beautiful SELF.

Sophia

Camellia Stadts

Ancient Hymns
Ancient Temples
Still ring with praise to
The Goddess Sophia.

She rises each morning as
The sun kisses the earth
She cradles us with her radiance
As the moon rises in soft slumber

Sophia, Goddess of Wisdom
So willing to share a
Gift too many find useless
Amidst concrete and steel

Brain power, man power
Clouds the skies, and minds
We can no longer see her beauty
Or feel her Grace, much less be
Silent enough to hear her wisdom

Can I know you, oh great Goddess
Of Wisdom who both rides the wind
And yet is the wind itself?

*"She is more beautiful than the sun and excels every
Constellation of the stars"* —Wisdom 7:29

We're All Goddesses

Pranada Comtois

I t took several years after beginning my practice of Bhakti yoga for some concepts to move beyond theory and take a place in my being. This isn't surprising since it's the nature of spiritual practice, or *sadhana*, to move from head-to-heart to become harmonized. One such concept, and perhaps one of the most provocative, is that all souls (whether in a male or female body) are feminine.

The feminine was oppressed in the community where I lived and in response, for a while, I tried to suppress my own femininity. Throughout those struggles I absorbed myself in *japa* and *kirtan*, the main practices of Bhakti yoga: Quietly to myself, and out loud in groups, respectively, I chanted the ancient Hare Krishna *maha*-mantra, which addresses the Supreme Divine as both male and female.

Although, at first my focus was on Krishna—the divine masculine—as my meditation progressed through the decades, Radha—the divine feminine and supreme Goddess—came to the forefront of my heart and awareness. Soon, pleasing her, serving her, and seeing her became my passionate, cherished goal.

As my practice continued, Radha revealed her beautiful qualities to me. She is patient, grave, affectionate, compassionate, gentle, grateful, merciful, respectful, etc. In fact, all souls possess the same goddess-like qualities at their spiritual cores. How I longed to awaken these within myself!

One text describes, "Radha is the full power, and Krishna is the possessor of full power." Gradually Radha, the Divine Feminine, showed me the formidable power of the feminine, for her love conquers the all-powerful Krishna! This divine vision of Goddess Radha overpowering God through love—knocking him off his throne—astonished me. I realized that the Goddess not only shares the throne at the summit of reality, she demurely controls it and he who owns it! And she does so with the deepest compassion and pure love: a love that drives God mad.

Each day my relationship with Radha—and understanding how powerful the feminine can be—deepens. Meditating on Goddess Radha has unlocked transcendental reflections in me as I begin to understand the awesome implications in declaring all souls as feminine: that we all have these qualities and this power of spiritual love, regardless of our biological genders. What a different world it would be if all people imbibed these powerful, divine qualities!

We experience masculine and feminine in this world—however imbalanced—because they have a pure state in the spiritual world. Unfortunately, our experiences of masculine and feminine energies are but impoverished reflections of their spiritual source and oftentimes the world subjugates the female and accentuates the male. The Goddess teaches us how to do away with inebriated concepts of gender by empowering ourselves with her divine qualities and her overpowering, pure love through service to our Divine Other.

This is the path of Bhakti, which I call "The Way of the Feminine Divine." It is the means by which we achieve our full potential as spiritual beings. It is the way of the Goddess of *Wise-Love*, Radha, unto whom I offer my life each day in the service of helping others call Radha into their lives.

Goddess Radha is the exemplar lover and the shelter of all affection. For me, she's the transcendent goal. Whether in a male or female body and whichever gender we identify with, in our spiritual perfection—according to Bhakti—we're all goddesses!

And what happens when we become divine goddesses in the truest sense? We become lovers. We conquer God! We conquer our Divine Other with our love. Is there any greater potential for the soul? Not as I see it.

Soften Her Steps

Chandrika McLaughlin

Krishna spoke:
She is love's power
That forces this shower
Of breath through my flute
To play a love song
Through the universe
And a balm to calm
The sufferings of earth.
She is the reason
For the lights to shine
In the luminaries of heaven
To be a sun or moon
Morning tune
As one sets the other rises
Captive to her glance
Where bewitched I dance
If only to capture
Her attention
For a moment that satisfies
Vast creation
Through the stunned hesitation
Of my heart
I would be the carpet of creepers
To soften her steps
Or the river of stars
To lift the lashes of her eyes
In wonder.
I am torn asunder
By her distress
When I travel far
And the fragments of me
Live in every cell and breath
of her life

And her tears
That call me back
Through each wrenching
Moment of separation
Of agony and ecstasy
That increases my unlimited love
Beyond all limits of tolerance
I play and dance for her pleasure
She is the treasure of all I see
And the entrance to me.

The Goddess Within

The Goddess doesn't enter us from outside; she emerges from deep within. She is not held back by what happened in the past. She is conceived in consciousness, born in love, and nurtured by higher thinking. She is integrity and value, created and sustained by the hard work of personal growth and the discipline of a life lived actively in hope.

Marianne Williamson

Rebirthing

Carolyn Riker

The woman in me is transforming. She's no longer a maiden. Her passages of motherhood have redefined her, filled her, and crafted her to be deeper. However, this middle space of aging is a bit confusing—she's no longer young and yet not too old, although she feels weathered and it has triggered a powerful rebirthing into a new layer of wholeness. Instead of carrying babes on hips and wiping tears of innocence, weight has crept there and aging has squeezed weeps into refined gold. In her searching, she's never fully alone and is more aware as she leans into listening; trees seem to gather nearer. She understands their whispers and feels a space of clover-dance, with mossy carpets and buttercups that seem to catch her glancing; she sees their small suns glowing through elder songs of grassy stories and evergreens reveal foretelling.

Her pages turn slower because her knees are swollen and cramping fingers need more time to restore between writing.

She notices the moon in all its phases. No one is better than the other. Howling only at the fullest makes her laugh because now she's free to howl whenever she so desires.

Her veins surge full of urgency at injustice, the raking over of femininity and lack of equality. She sees her unearned white skin and presses her voice to be bolder and sometimes louder. It's a struggle to stand tall because saplings think they know better.

But it's not true.

Maturity is drenched in a condensation of salty perseverance. The sea flows over granite arms feathered soft, now airborne to weather any storm. She knows time spent dormant is a learned refuge.

The woman in me is transforming into the goddess she never knew.

In Her Kingdom
Sandra M. Allagapen

She giggles in my mind
The child within
Her innocence unbound
Sounds like wind chimes in the breeze
She is joy without frontiers

She dances with abandon
The wild woman within
She knows that she holds the key
To a universe that sparkles anew
She is the rainbow after the storm

She meanders through my soul
The wise woman within
Offering new choices each day
To reach beyond fear and claim love
She is the smell of Earth after the rain

She rides in on thunder
The warrior within
Ready to slay all threats
To the soft-hearted and the kind
She wears justice as her crown

She treads carefully
The artist within
Unaware of the magic she wields
Even as it restores my spirit
She can create a new world each day

She glows with each prayer
The heart within
Every wound, a fissure

That she fills with gold
She is the transformer

She walks silently
The mother within
A loving touch here
An encouraging whisper there
Her strength is compassion

She moves with grace
The Goddess within
As she dances with the wild woman
And sings to the child
She soothes the warrior
After listening to the wise woman
She embraces the heart
And nurtures the artist
When peace finally prevails
She sits in silence
In the sacredness of the divine heart
Where only love matters
And where she rules

The Goddess in Me

Maureen Lancaster

I searched
amongst
the stars,
the woods,
the waters
and the hard
concrete of life
for her

the one
with whom I
would sit at
her feet and
admire
her strength,
her courage,
her tenacity,
her wisdom,
and would
glean
from her
all that
I could

I searched
amongst
the faces
that passed
by me each
and every day

I searched
amongst

the voices
heard within
the wind as
it brushed
by my face

I searched
amongst
the words
inked by
those thought
so much wiser
than I

I searched
until that
fateful day
when passing
by a mirror
did I see
a Goddess
in human form
who looked
just like me

I searched
until I found
that inside
did reside
this Warrior,
this Queen,
this Woman
that I was,
just patiently
waiting to
be seen...

The Return of the Goddess

Samiel Carolina

She left us, not eradicated by men, but eradicated by women themselves.

Many generations ago, women left...

... their bodies, so they could survive in a world ruled by the mind.
... the moon, to work in a world where intellectual knowledge was much more important than life experience-based wisdom.
... their cycles, so they could function and belong in a world that understood time in a linear way.
... the Earth, so they could find refuge, comfort and order in this man-made world.

In that world of the mind, knowledge and linear time is dead.

When we look around, we have the proof:

... our physical bodies are ill, lacking ease of movement.
... our mind is depressed, lacking purpose.
... our illusion of linear time creates alienation.
... our Earth is polluted, losing her aliveness, her various species and her magic.

The Goddess must return. In fact, she is already here.

She is here through each woman who chooses exquisite self-care practices to nourish herself at a deep Soul level. The Goddess helped her to remember that she can only give to others what first she gives to herself.

She is here through each woman who returns to the magic of nourishing her family and community with homemade recipes, infusing her cooking with her humor, love and devotion. The Goddess guided her to honor her own body and that of those she loves, as a temple that deserves to be well nourished for health and aliveness.

She is here through each woman who performs simple acts of peace and harmony by making herself and her home beautiful. The Goddess whispered in her ear that beauty is her birthright, that simplicity soothes the mind and invites the Soul back in.

She is here through each woman who shares her most vulnerable stories of pain and joy with her tribe, and with strangers. The Goddess granted her the courage and beauty of an open heart.

The Goddess, for me, is in each one of us. I do not experience her as something outside or bigger than myself; rather, I experience her in my inspiration, in the silence inside my head, in the beauty around me, in lovemaking, in nature, in animals, all creation and of course, in my intuition.

She comes to me as the big divine cosmic fire that burns and transmutes back into ashes of love all the ignorance that is still here from the old world.

This is the cosmic fire that ignites our dreams and fuels our courage to make them reality. This is the fire that helps us to remember we have chosen this lifetime to bring the Goddess back on Earth, through our bodies, minds and hearts.

I connect to her mostly in silence, an internal silence, while I am in movement or still, working or playing, cooking or making love.

When I am not willing to listen, and I would rather try to control my life, she comes and kicks my ass so strongly; I have learned to really pay attention to my intuition, and the signs I constantly receive. She really is a badass kind of woman, full of love and ready to burn what is not true so that beauty can rise from the ashes.

I prefer to surrender and be guided by her. She taught me that my personality is not what I am here for. She helps me to remember my Soul's dreams. At times overwhelmed by the enormous task I am here to leave as a legacy, sometimes I think I would rather quit, as my ancestors did.

She's the one who comes in those moments of alienation to help me remember that all she wants is for me to be JOYFUL. I relax then, and finally accept and embrace my Soul's task again: my goddess essence.

It is in each one of us. It is in you, too.

The Original and Eternal Shakti

Dolly Mahtani

I once heard a story. It's more of a legend, really. It spoke of a golden age called *satya yuga*: the era of truth—the purest period of time during the cycle of the world. At that time, a magical ball was held. A grand ball! Kings and queens, princes and princesses were paired up to rule the kingdom. So there was a dance, a special dance, one in which everyone moved according to their own rhythm, to the song in their soul. (This is my favorite part!) It is said that the dancers at this ball picked their match through *drishti*, an elevated practice of soul-to-soul vision, the piercing of another's eyes to recognize the soul behind the glance. It was a time in which just one look was enough to know if your hearts should be bound to each other! Bodies, habits, and values had nothing to do with it. Instead, it involved a magnetic recognition at a metaphysical level. Once the dancers were coupled, plans for a royal wedding unfolded, in preparation for them to rule the kingdom for eternity.

I fell in love with this story because, to me, it felt like the truth: to participate in love, all we need to do is recognize it! This is also what the Goddess means to me: connecting to that eternal energy of love that exists within us all. I believe that as a result of being disconnected from this, we all carry a deep longing within us, a gaping hole that nothing around us can seem to fill. This hole is deep-rooted. Ancient. Older than any religion! I know this longing well. It is fueled by my memory of the age of purity and truth: of *satya*, of a time when I—Goddess-like—ruled over a happy and joyous kingdom. And in this memory, I am not alone, but next to someone. I am always next to someone, sharing love. Though I can't tell you who this someone is, I carry in me the longing left by this person's absence—this person whose presence I shared for millennia. This is why my life plays itself out like a search for this person: my own eternal dance partner, my goddess energy, my *Shakti*, the *real* me.

Shakti is an identity beyond the ego's reach. It is the truth of who I am, embodying all my experiences. Even my suffering, my

148

pain and my sadness have a purpose now: they show me that I am disconnected from my *shakti*. Such moments of hopelessness and despair become unique opportunities for me to awaken, to remember who I am and where I came from. My emptiness gives me space to reconnect to the deeper me. And I don't need to be filled. It's not a matter of *becoming* a Goddess, it's a matter of remembering that I've always been one. For stirring within me I feel a Ceres, Isis, Lakshmi, Athena, Aphrodite, Artemis, Kali, Hera, Durga, Parvati and Saraswati!

Once I adopt this new consciousness, I understand that I'm letting the old one go. With the death of my old identity come new vision, new focus, new thoughts, new words, and new actions. *Shakti* energy starts to flow through me, around me, spilling over into every aspect of my life and transforming everything around me! This doesn't happen gradually. It's more of a quantum leap in which I suddenly become an instrument in service of the love that I am. I cannot be selfish or have attachments. I cannot feel jealousy or consider myself the victim of any situation. I am a powerful, pure, beautiful and original being. I ground myself in this eternal truth. My truth. Now I have access to my unlimited creativity, beauty and intuition! With it, I help create a new world, one that reflects the reign of the original and eternal Shakti within each of us. So seek her out; she wants to dance with you!

A Poet's Inclination

Kai Coggin

A poet's inclination,
I open my heart up so much
that it sometimes takes in whole galaxies,
I swallowed three moons before it was noon
inside me they are orbiting a new sun,
there are no secrets,
nothing is too much for words,
there is a poem in this moment,
I can feel it, can't you?

There are no mountaintops that do not hold my name,
I am covered in sand, scratched into the earth.
There is not a sky that I have not breathed
and gathered in and pushed away
and flown into with colors gripped in my teeth,
this expanse lives inside
yet I am easily lost in my own circles.
There is not a sound
that I have not rocked against my naked chest,
told that it was mine to hold
until death becomes life again,
told that I would give it another sound to marry
under my tongue and they would dance and dance.
Sounds are a world of their own, you know?

I want to love every woman that I meet,
tell her that she is the muse that frequents my dreams,
and that it is her face that makes me believe
there is such a thing as sunrise,

but I just put all of that wanting into these poems,
these countless lines that define existence from my point of sky,
through the eye of a beholder that beholds her with rhymes,
I write these hyperboles,
pour out these lines into an abyss of white
and give them my last name,
marry me,
it is natural to want permanence
when everything changes,
when there is nothing to pin down
except the hopes that there will be no more pins,

I have broken every mold that I
have thought to put myself in, hand, cage, border, page.
Everyday, I am born again.
Today, I am an infant and tomorrow still.
If my hands become sponges, I can soak it all in
and remember to forget it all when I go to sleep,
remember to pronounce every star
before counting all the sheep,
let me have it,
let me take this to the apex of someone's burning question,
become water for me, world,
fill me with the absence of you becoming desert,
make me an ocean of your movement
and I will become the tide at dusk and the tide at dawn,
there is never too much rising, I say.

There is never too much rising.

Milk & Moonshadows

A.B Cooper

Standing naked,
Bathed in milky moonlight,
Murmur of night breeze
Kisses damp skin.
Gelatin silver contrast shadows reveal
Shifted landscapes:
New peaks jut proudly,
Others subsiding.
I cradle hot flesh,
Relieve the rock hard heaviness.

Sleeping shape senses my presence,
Smells me,
Stirs.
We cling stickily,
Bathed in sweat.
Nuzzling skin
Darkened by Sister Sun.

Familiar bittersweet prickle
Floods.
Deep draw:
I overflow,
Rivers of silver cascading down peaks and gullies.

Tiny fingers spasm involuntarily,
Eyes rolling in milk-drunk stupor,
Breathing slows with
Soporific sighs...

I am nourishment.
I comfort.
I am peace.
I am Goddess.

(This poem first appeared in an online pamphlet with Paper Swans Press, 2014, Issue 2)

I am Woman
Rebecca DeLeo

I am Mother Earth, the Creatrix.
I am the Mother of the Cosmos, the High Priestess.
The gateway to God lies between my towering pillars of ecstatic surrender.
The brine of scarlet, flowing from my sap-soaked temple, is an ever-nourishing spring of esoteric wisdom.
My elixirs, furiously coursing through my monstrance of beat and pounce, are the nectars of eternal life.
Part the Red Sea, and dissolve into your Dark Mother.
Drink from me, for I am the Fountain of Youth.
Feed on my ripe fruits, for my womanhood is your source of life.
Cascade into me;
I am the raging inferno that ravages your ravenous soul.
Lose yourself in the Womb of the World;
You are mine to devour.
In me, you disintegrate to reemerge.
I am She who gives you life;
I am She who gives you death.
I am the Maiden, the Waxing Moon.
I am the Mother, the Full Moon.
I am the Enchantress, the Waning Moon.
I am the Crone, the Dark Moon.
I am the Sacred Whore, the Holy Harlot.
I am the Seer, the Illuminatrix.
I am the Dark Goddess, the Veiled Mother of Mystery.
I am the Great Giver and the Great Receiver.
I am the Daughter of Dawn and the Mother of Dusk.
I am the Shekinah.
I am Shakti.
I am Woman.

Impossibilities

Shannon Crossman

The Divine
thrums inside
my heart like
the steady beat
of dragonfly wings
against wind,
all gossamer and
improbable yet,
no less real.

My mouth
aches with
stories to spill
from lips that
bit into
possibility and
tasted the
ineffable.

How to express
the inexplicable
nature of being
ripe with
the Divine?

A most profound
pregnancy, forever
gestating. One long
threaded strand and
many millions of
tiny births.

Impossible? Yes,
and yet, no less
real.

She Begins To Rise

Cheryl Anne Bratman

I spoke Her Name
aloud today;
the Old One inside,
Who, even now, is
Where I Am Going.

And in my speaking,
Strength rose up,
Grace poured down,
Wisdom wrapped round
about; a Sacred Mantle.

Lovingly, She
in me spoke in turn,
"You've much to learn
and to discern along the Path
to this Place I hold for you,
but do not fear for I
have cleared the Way."

It's a comfort,
how She knows me
and shows me how
to see myself aright.

It's a blessing
how She loves me
through all my false starts
and cradles my heart:

patient and tender
as a Nursing Mother
Whose little one
can't quite seem to latch on.

I spoke Her Name
aloud today;
the Old One
Who kindles my flames
and pulls my tides,
Who stands my ground
and teaches me to fly.

Keeper of my Inner Elements.

And in my speaking,
I saw through Her
Old Eyes,
Looking back
and forward all at once,
This Moment of Grace—
The Holy Place,
Where I rest
and She begins to rise.

Sometimes
Janavi Held

Sometimes I am all of them!
Aphrodite
and the woman
who craved the sea
and sprouted gills at night,
whose hair turned to seaweed,
the woman with red-earth running in her veins
and gold sunlight knitting her hair together.
And
sometimes
I am such an ordinary woman
taking up little room
walking unnoticed
inside a shell
of space
and skin.
I don't last long without seaweed in my hair
those days roll by
collapsing me
on top of
me.
I am the woman running free at night
unable to breathe without the full force of the wind
liberating the fallen arches of my heart.
I was the girl who dreamed of magic.
Now
a woman
with empty hands
I spin this magical tapestry
from the golden threads
birthing inside my chest
keeping
my life
together.

Her Voice

Mandy Adams

As a young woman, I was fascinated to learn that there was a Goddess and that her myriad forms could reveal to me the many parts of myself. I was particularly struck during my travels to India, where I observed that each Hindu Goddess had her own equal God as consort, and her own accompanying power animal or 'transport.' I watched young couples offer flowers to *yonis* and *lingams* in temples there and saw a very different honoring of both the feminine and the masculine principles. It was a stark contrast to what I had been brought up with in my own British culture and it stirred something deep within me.

In my life, I have experienced times of deep presence and during these cherished moments I have been aware of an inner voice inside of me. The voice is both gentle and powerfully loud —and now as I grow older it is becoming increasingly persistent. I have come to name this inner voice of guidance Her voice—I hear it as the voice of the Earth / The Goddess because it is wise beyond my knowing. Often it reveals my next steps with great certainty, as well as those I need to contact and those I need to spend time with and learn from. At times, it is accompanied by lucid dreams and visions of past, present and future colliding. At others, it is friendly reminder to come back home to my own self-care and inner nourishment, especially so when Life has propelled me so far from my centre that there is a risk of separation or abandonment from Her guidance.

I have most felt Her presence when I am alone, in nature, am able to be still, and especially during my menstruation. I have also felt Her during group circle work, where there has been enough trust, honesty and holding for our inner landscapes to be revealed. In these settings, I feel myself becoming whole again. I watch myself seeing each part of me come to life in the story of another. These parts I have often witnessed as the many faces of the Goddesses and Gods that I have come to know throughout my life. I have a bone-deep knowing that this is how we, as indigenous peoples, would have practiced keeping our tribes whole and staying in balance with the Land that has nourished us.

I am a woman whose family has lived in the same part of Cornwall, in the far Southwest of the British Isles, for as far back as records can trace. My work has taken me to a deepening practice and understanding of the menstrual cycle. Here I can observe in my own body the cyclical rising and falling energy that governs all living things on our beautiful Earth. This monthly rhythm that moves through us can be compared with the seasons of nature. Our menstruation can be likened to the drawing in and deep rest and visioning that Winter brings; our pre-ovulation to the emerging and newly sprouting energies of Spring; our ovulation akin to the high energy of Summer and full capacity to hold all that life brings, and our pre-menstrum to the energy of Autumn's harvest, slowing down and preparing for Winter again.

These seasonal energies that govern us each month can also be seen as the life cycle of a woman. The Spring represents the Maiden or innocent, playful, loving and sexual part of ourselves. The Summer represents the Mother who nurtures and holds, the warrioress, the destructive and creative part of ourselves. The Autumn represents the Marga or all-seeing high priestess, the *sha-mana*, or magically intuitive part of ourselves, and the Winter represents the Crone or wise elder, guide, companion and sovereign part of ourselves. All four quadrants reveal each aspect of woman as Goddess in her many forms. Each week we encounter one of Her faces governing and speaking through us.

> *"Each Inner Season holds a key initiatory step, or stage, that works you month after month through your menstruating years in order to become and claim your full self"*—Alexandra Pope and Sjanie Hugo Wurlitzer, *"Wild Power—discover the magic of your menstrual cycle and awaken the feminine path to power,"* p.54.

As I watch and consciously track which aspects of Her I repress—or put away into shadow out of grief, anger or fear of claiming my full self—I seek the support of other women also watching their inner cycle and the outer expression of that cycle which they have created in their lives. I am convinced that as we each share how we hear Her voice throughout our monthly cycle, that we are restoring the way that indigenous peoples the world over would have met and practiced reverence for all Life.

As I close, I am reminded of the young couples laying flowers on the *yonis* and *lingams* in the temples in India I witnessed long ago. Women's bodies, and in particular menstruation, have long been shamed and considered to be taboo. Here in this shamefully despised, covered, hidden and physically and emotionally painful place, I have heard Her voice, and in doing so I am finding the courage to claim my own. May this commitment to restoring my cyclical nature flow over to my husband and in turn, our three sons.

Dancing With Roots in the Spring
Emelina Holland

Bury my feet deep into the ground Divine Mother,
so that I can grow roots that connect me to your core.
May I be love to all I encounter Divine Mother,
like the tree spirit that guides and feeds my soul.
May I grow tall, wide and abundant
while expanding in wisdom
wide and deep down too.
May I always blossom and be fruitful,
colorful and vibrant,
while loving and honoring
the cycles of my body's tunes.
May I honor and embrace the wisdom
of my Falls and Winters
for the sacred times of quiet rest
and Divine contemplation they gift to me.
May I always give life to all I touch
and to all that touches me Divine Mother...
May my heart always shine
like a radiant and eternal Summer
even during the nights while my body sleeps.
May I always live long grounded and with you Divine Mother,
like the enduring
still standing ancient trees...
So that I can see the sun and let him touch me every morning...
So I can dance and sing to the full moon all of the dreams I
breathe...
So that I can feel the white snow when is falling,
and the whispering wind when caressing my skin.
So that I can hear the stars reciting me poems
and the afternoon skies showing me stories.
I want to continue to be love through all of my senses
and to make love with all that I think and feel...
So please!

Bury my feet deep down into the ground Divine Mother,
so I can grow roots
that keep me standing humble and strong
with faithful bright rebirths,
celebrating the Spring dance of my soul's song
even when I may find myself standing alone.

Elemental

Durdica Maderic

Wild, Whole and Immense
She is timeless, boundless Being
She doesn't live according to masculine prescriptions
Or time restrictions
She flows according to her own rhythm and harmonics
Guided by her inner compass
In touch with her elemental being
She takes care of her deepest and most immediate needs
She lets the season blend with her body
She lets the elements stir a bit within her
She watches her waters flow abundantly

She allows the wind to blow through the old cobwebs
Release the old structures
So that she may gather herself a bit deeper and wider
Weave the new webs of stronger and more solid connections, a
Portal of new perspectives
She allows herself to soften and sink into the ground of her being
Rest and conserve her energy
Reflect without pressure to produce, strive or try harder
She allows the fire to warm her cold and tired bones
To consume her burn down her ailments
Surrender to the delights of her heart's desires

In this safe temple
In this space of self-preservation and self-validation
She recreates herself again and again
Inspired and guided by new passions
Inevitably much happens for her in such dark, fertile and still cavern
Being, dreaming, hibernating, pausing before taking new breaths
When she accepts the loving embrace of Dark Mother
She is initiated into simplicity and effortlessness of her
nature rhythm

Her flesh relaxed,
In the space of inhaling and exhaling
She knows she is home.

The Divine and Dirty Goddess
Aislen Hartwell

You will not find my Goddess in perfect and orderly shrines. Nor will you find her genuflecting and obsequious.

She is a Holy Riot, there in the open, for all of us to see. Unabashed and shameless, Her breeze will cool your brow while Her storms quicken your pulse. She is there in the sweat and stillness, the dirt, as well as the sun.

My Goddess is not and cannot be separate from me. She is the child that one day grows to bear her own children. We see Her offspring, a glorious bounty that stems from the dark and fecund womb of She.

You want to see life, yes? Come then, seek the dark. Reach and embrace those places of mud, shadow, and sludge. Prepare for the blindness that is Endarkenment, a place not just of 'not knowing,' but of Unknowing.

My Goddess is with me when heart and mind are torn asunder. My Goddess demands sacrifice, the old in exchange for the new. She wants to see how well I die, what I've learned, and how I handle my own sacred mess. Do I water my life with the Holy Sacraments of women—blood, sweat, and tears? What light do I shine on my Holy Chaos? Sun, and moon, or only sixty watts?

My Goddess is with me when the vodka bottle calls over the yoga mat, for She too, in all Her multitudes, has known savagery, heartbreak, and fear. Along with Her daughters, She has been raped, shattered, and sacrificed. My Goddess screams and wails, having to bear witness to the soul-numbing and womb freezing that is man's inhumanity to man.

Our Goddess is there for us when we flee houses built upon rage and injustice. Cloaking us in silent footfalls and trembling will, She protects us as we run into the night, not knowing if we will live to see another day. She is there when we say "NO! NO MORE!" casting off from abusive relationships. We then set sail on obsidian seas, through the Dark Night of our Soul.

Bruises, scrapes, scars, and burns, these are the very places that the Goddess shall kiss over and over until She and We are One. Every unjust touch is a tear in the very fabric of She.

You see, we are not just Holy after baths, candles, and incense. It is in tears and snot, blood and scars that the true strength of our Goddess is shown. So let dirt cake your precious feet and nest under your ferocious nails. Let sweat erase our made up faces and have Our own blood cover us, unrepentant, from groin to ass. We are, after all, made in Her image:

The Divine and Dirty Goddess.

Veneration of the Wild Witch
Jennifer R. Miller

There are two witches living inside of me... one wild, one tame. I won't deny that I love the wild one most—

She who resists order and structure, she who prefers the loamy smell of woodlands and the sand of untrodden shores, she who calls the lightning bolt down to shatter the tower, she who gives not a single flying fuck about your opinions.

The wild witch knew magic long before it was sifted down and spread categorically into the pages of dusty books and grimoires. She knew it well before the Golden Dawn, before Gardner, before Cunningham, before replicated lists and correspondence tables. She knew the Goddess before they gave her names and the Horned Hunter before they demonized him.

The wild witch walked in the forest, lifted her hands to the sky and felt the radiance of the noonday sun pulsing through her veins. She pulled the power of rocks and soil and gnarly roots up through her bare feet into the core of her being, renewing her connection to the Earth Mother. She waded into the stream, and the water swirling about her calves and thighs was her very first lover.

The trees spoke to her in every season, bearing the changes of growth and dormancy in equal measure; so she learned to do the same, dropping her leaves like the oak in autumn... blooming like the hawthorn in spring. The flowers and herbs beckoned to her, revealing all of their secrets one by one, and they became her strongest allies. Rosemary grew tall and strong at her door. Artemisia graced the entry to her garden. Primrose danced between the stones of her walkway.

The wild witch attended the university of the winged ones, the four-leggeds, and the creepy crawlies. Lessons arrived daily. She listened to the hawk's piercing cry and reveled in the raucous laughter of crows...caught a glimpse of the elusive fox and the owl's golden eyes at dusk...watched the shy, gentle deer and the steely serpent shedding its skin.

The moon waxes and wanes, and so does the wild witch.

The cycle of

Intentions
Expansions
Culminations
Reflections
Releasings

replays over and over again with the ebb and flow of Luna.

Her world is fearless inspiration... blood and fire of creation... bitter ashes of death and destruction.

She recoils from domestication.

Don't try to "save" her, please. You will find her in the deepest of caves, drawing portraits of her yoni on the walls with red ochre.

The wild witch loves as only feral beings can love... completely but without attachment, deeply but without anchors.

There are two witches living inside of me... one wild, one tame... and how fiercely I love the wild one.

My Feral Heart

Catherine L. Schweig

After she woke,
I let her go wonderfully wild
much to the chagrin of cranky neighbors.
I shooed away their goats
until pastures sprouted woodlands,
and the grasses wore bouncy, pine-needle coats.

I let her green lawns turn to thicket
impervious to their complaints.
Closed my gate on their hunting hounds
until rabbits burrowed, and moles thrived
and she became a midwife to many, happy fawns.

I watched her turn savage:
until mating raptors nested in her limbs,
arachnid silks decorated her untamed hair
the prowling lynx hunted on her soft mounds.

I smelled her floral festivals in spring,
licked her blackberry juice off my fingers,
felt the little creek overflow in summer,
let the snakes swim in her pond.

I watched her undress to the bone:
Her Maple skeletons shivering under Northern gales
obsolete garments tossed off in colorful spurts
to the scattering of crows, the cooing of doves,
the pleasant panting of autumn.

I heard her sigh on misty, winter mornings
just after daylight had silenced the owls
veiled in velvety moss and magic
wrapped in scented shawls of dew and delight.

And I felt her beckoning me insistently
on bright nights, ripe for howling,
into her nooks, and crannies, and wings
where my feral heart would roam,
and ravenously feed,
after she woke.

The Wild Woman

Gloria D. Gonsalves

There is a call from the frightened place
daring my scared feet to feel the wet mud
running to where the moon flirts with bare skin
and walking a path caressed by uncombed hair.

A dwelling where rules and walls disappear
except stories, poetry and songs of the spirit
bones freed of fearful and belittling shackles
a soul in charge of its own dance through life.

Tonight I will get out and run to the woods
to bathe in the full moon and get rid of my shadows
to sing and recite until fear accepts defeat
then return home, knowing how to flee.

a goddess of song
Linda M. Crate

so many grey days,
but there's still
light;
so i know that there is goodness
left in this world
i will unearth it with every spell
of my love
nature reminds me some of the prettiest things
are buried in plain sight—
i can find the dreaming in flowers,
rivers, creeks, stones,
trees, the songs of birds, wishing wells,
and anywhere the light touches
because we are all broken
in some way;
it's how the light comes in and refurbishes
our dreams
each of our stories weaves a beautiful tapestry,
and each one of us possesses the
power to be goddesses
all we must do is unleash our fears and our doubts
overthrow our insecurities and realize our
magic—
we are all powerful,
and i refuse to be tamed or told to sit upon a pretty
pedestal because no pretty cage could ever
steal my song;
my psalm is only for those whom deserve it.

She

Cheryl Anne Bratman

She is
deep, leafy green,
moist earthen brown,
petal-soft pink.

Clay, bronze,
mother-of-pearl,
warm blooded flesh
on Ecstasy's brink.

She is
within me
and Everywhere I turn—
in passions that burn

and clear
cooling tears,
empathizing, empowering
abolishing fear.
Beyond mere symbol;

flame or dove.
She has no equal
and bows to none but Love.

Gaia Voice and
The Empowered Woman
Leah Salomaa

One of the things I enjoy most in life is the experience of contrast: the opposites in life. As a kid I used to love getting dirty, then bathing and feeling all clean. I would also enjoy getting a cold and resting, only to feel better and even healthier than I was before. Such extremes cut through monotony and predictability: sensations I have always disliked. Instead, I love the sensation of working hard—through the struggles, through the darkness—and enjoying the big, unexpected payoff.

It's been my experience, as a professional singer and voice trainer, that we cannot experience the opening of our true hearts and crown chakras—full of sacred tones—without going to the dark places first. We cannot sit in a sacred circle community and support other sisters without looking at our own emotional shadows first. In short, a sacred Gaia voice is an authentic voice that incorporates even the darkness.

To me, empowering women to use their Gaia voices is all about expansion, and embracing the experience of contrast and extremes. To be addicted to light, love and happiness actually constricts the throat and voice to a place of fake tones. But to expand yourself and go deep within—roar in your darkness and listen to others as they curse their way through their truth—here is where the sweetness lives. We surrender to the real as we excavate through the mine of stories we have let pile up in our bellies of who we 'think' we are.

What happens when we try to make our voices sound the way we 'think' they should sound? What happens when we yearn for a sacred experience singing with our pure voice, but then human emotions get in the way? What happens when we, as women on a journey longing for sacred communion, sit in a circle with others only to find that there is some messy energy there getting in the way of experiencing sweet light and bliss? So many of the students I work with ask these questions in their urge to bypass the emotional body—and the ugly voices within them—and to go straight to the sweetness. But this only leads to frustration, and maybe even to becoming stuck in the process.

When we become stuck in our lives, our Gaia voices, or sacred voices, become stuck too. This is when it's time to relax, and sit in this place for a while. So, instead, we practice breathing through the anger and the impulse to self-criticize. We trust that everything is sacred, even our struggles. We understand that every single one of us carries our own "shit" and that there is no shame in this. Still, it gets stuck in our throats, our nervous stomachs, our chronic headaches, lower back pain and sinus infections, so we need sifting, purging, and releasing. When we allow ourselves not to bypass this important step, we are rewarded with the contrasting sensation of sweetness.

So the Gaia power that you will ultimately feel in your voice doesn't come from anger; it doesn't even come from pure love and light. To me—in what I have witnessed in my own voice journey and teaching others to sing and vocalize their truth—it comes from this real place of holy communion between Darkness and Light, which then becomes an open conduit to Source/God/the Goddess: Ultimate LOVE.

Yes, I believe that the world was created from a deep place of LOVE. I believe that every human comes into the world with the ability and need to experience and receive LOVE. As I write this, it is the beginning of spring in London, Ontario, Canada, and all the wildlife is beaming with the love of being alive! The creatures are not questioning if they've got the birdsong right or if they're growing their tree trunks properly. They are divinely woven into the pulsing heartbeat of Gaia, Mother Earth and the Great Spirit that supports them.

Well, we are all part of that fabric. We are Divinely loved and needed in this song of creation. Our breath is supported by the blood of generations tied to the oceans and the mountains of the land, and the stars of the heavens. Sounds a bit grand, but aren't we?

So, what if we breathe from this place? What if we sing with the love from this place? What if we walk through our lives from this place? What if we all released our powerful Gaia voices into the world? What an experience of contrast that would be! The power of our authentic truth riding on the sweetness of pure creation!

I believe it's in all of us to sing our own song and rise together.

Harvest Moon

Debra Hall

I have a Venus urge
for autumn cooking, slow lovemaking;
spiced apples, root crumbles, soft kisses, chunky pickles,
smooth languorous caresses.
My grateful love for you.
The mild sun beckons me outside
to pick up hazel nuts from the warm afternoon track,
to make us wisdom cake.
My body is soft like the after glow of pleasure and late summer.
Indigo black berries, dark scarlet rowans and
a startling show of purple-blue sloes in the spiked hedgerows
have deepened the years palette, even further.
Steeped in gin, the sloes will make a sweet, tart toast
to the returning sun at Midwinter.
I could put the whole day into my mouth,
swallow the circling buzzard's plaintive shadow and
soar above the ridge, singing with my voice free
in more colors than the leaves are falling.
In delighted rhapsody my creatures unwind,
I applaud their grace.
Later as the harvest moon births herself slowly... lavishly...
immoderately... capaciously... sybaritically from the far hill,
a Goddess slides from my body,
twirling infinity belly dances
out of the kitchen door.

Coconut

Tosha Silver

don't tell me
how well you conjure
dream
or list your wishes
for ghosts to grant
on Full Moons
or how you
manifested your mate
in a month
or that parking space
in a jam
or how you always get
whatever you want
whenever you want it
cuz I still
don't care.
You can spend a whole life
chasing This
or That
when instead
You could be
a coconut
cracked by
God's own hand
and splashed
on this earth
like holy
milk

I Found Me

Alyscia Cunningham

The wail of demise,
Signals weary cries of grief,

I close my eyes and strive to ignore the belief,
Of an insecure trait for relief.

They've robbed me of sleep,
The outcomes are deep,
As I force not to reap,
The sorrowful fruits they weep.

How can they not see?
Abuse is far from free,
Rather than flee,
Hitting her hurt me.

My silence evolved into offense,
Guarding my space and presence,
I built a fence,
Armored with reactive self-defense.

I strived not to repeat,
but became a cheat,
Numbing possible defeat,
My movements swayed discrete.

Feeding traits of deceit,
To fulfill the less concrete.

Not realizing that compressing,
Was expressing,
Through a shattered dressing.

And in all, the unseen blessing,
Was revealed through my progressing.

It took some time for me to see,
The Goddess in me.

So, I chose to break free,
Trusting my journey, cleared debris,
And in that process, I found me.

Reclamation Song
Jhilmil Breckenridge

Too black. Too white. Too straight. Too gay.
Too Hindu. Too middle class. Too thin.
Too fat. Too loud. Too quiet. Too.

Language assaults my body. And I bleed.
I bleed rivers and I wade through my own blood.
I cry; my single cry echoing with the cries

of a hundred sisters, huddled, waiting.
My cry is the echo of every woman shamed.
My cry is the memory of every girl child killed.

And still they speak. Too trans. Too sexual.
Too frigid. Too much. Too little.
Too.

Language assaults my body.
My body is home and I am chopped up
into a million pieces.

And as the echoes get louder, the blood
is a roar in my ears. I hear the *dholak*.
I smell the fire. I see the vermilion at her brow.

Too sexy. Too fat. Too loud.
And my hips are dancing as I laugh.
My body reclaimed as I feel my ancestors,

hearing only music, only the rhythm,
the scent of *mogra*.
And I am home. I am finally home.

Her Ancient Hymns
Sonja Phillips

She is awakening to the songs of her inner goddess.
She is learning to dance in her own darkness.
She is chanting a new song, daring to be different.
Beneath the quieted moon, undisturbed.
Lost in the ancient hymns of her.
I hear a voice that is mine, and another.
A timeless rhythm, within the depths of my soul.
I came to know her.
We are one in nature.
Her, the other within.
She has taken me to a place of solace,
the deep inner knowing that lives within me,
I wish never to return, reclaiming the power once held by her.
Her divine light is emerging,
the goddess has returned.
From her lips to my heart.
Her best intentions are kindled by something
more than flesh can touch,
more than words can obtain,
She is lifting us into the highest forms of love.
She is wounded but loves so deeply.
Estranged from the gods, her love diminishes not.
She sings on, resurrecting the Eden within herself.
I hear the song of a goddess.
Aligning with the inner rhythms of nature.
Aligning with the soft anthems of the sky.
I can hear the musical intonations of the universe in her being.
Her enchanting music uniting the inner and outer realms.
Beneath the quieted moon, undisturbed,
a universal song of love.
Lost in the ancient hymns of her.
My inward journey is just a
wandering home.

Who Is She?

Lucy H. Pearce

I realize, looking back, that She fully awoke within me when I was just about to turn sixteen. She pulsed shamelessly through my body—in my desire, in my voice, in my blossoming beauty and most of all in my art. She spilled onto the page in symbols I only half recognized—priestesses disguised as flamenco dancers and bird women. The symbolism of the egg, the flower, the fish, the bridge to beyond. She was initiating me without my even knowing it. I felt alive on the deepest level. Everything flowed. I was bright and brilliant and brave and beautiful and full with Her. Without knowing of or naming Her, She was there. And I was She. She was not a matter of belief.

And then suddenly the magic disappeared. The loss of my first lover and the death of my beloved grandmother created a whirlwind of disconnection. A feeling of desperate aloneness in a cold world that didn't understand what flowed through me. The terror that if I opened my mouth and trusted the flow that rather than butterflies and golden magic, frogs would jump out. It was no coincidence that I felt had a frog in my throat that blocked the way. I was consumed by the fear of what would emerge if I opened my mouth. If I opened my legs. What if nothing came out? Or everything did? A dance of divine darkness and sacred honey lay within, but it felt too unsafe to come out through this body. This female body. And so I shut it away. Shaking and silent. And sad.

I can remember when I last felt this way: I was three, laying in a hammock, nearly naked in the sunshine and dappled shade, in the warm breeze, the gentle sway, the safe wild beauty of my grandmother's garden. The golden honey feeling of Her permeates this memory of blissful belonging. I was connected to life force. She was me, and I was She. And then the blockage at the throat. The sickness, the terror and trauma of safety being ripped away.

This has happened many times. The connection. The honey light. The flow of pleasure and joy through my body. The feeling of complete belonging to life, of being an intimate channel of magical power. And then all this followed by terror. And dark disconnection. And sad loneliness. And me shutting down.

I look again and see that this happened at each significant threshold in my life. Each major step has held this energetic key: first, the move into childhood. Next, moving into womanhood. Then, moving into motherhood, followed by the move into *Womancraft.* Looking back, each phase seems like a portal into divine feminine initiation. I start with pure connection to Her. A deep, trusted, unspoken connection. A flow. A knowing. A feeling so right in my skin. A feeling of being home.

No one gave me the words for it. I simply lived it, and knew it to my depths. This was my truth. In the world beyond me, I was surrounded by stories of kings and gods and big brother and The Man. But She was my own living gospel. My private knowing, as opposed to my adopted, enforced beliefs.

But as real and true and natural as She is, as my knowing is, I lose it time and again. A forced forgetfulness fueled by shame. Torn away by the world. She is a victim of a head-on collision with patriarchal reality. She is burned and tarred and feathered and ridiculed and dismissed so easily that I wonder if perhaps I imagined Her. Dreamed Her. Wished Her to be true.

But I think the greater truth is that they sensed her power and wished Her away. Forced Her away. Tore Her away.

I go back to the beginning of this body, this life: The forceps delivery, the enforced end of breastfeeding. I was not in charge of each of these first instances of tearing apart. It may be a habit I repeat unconsciously now. But the first times were not my doing. The severing from Her was done to me. Forcibly. From my mother, from my Mother. But at each new stage, I pass through a doorway that connects directly to Her, and for a moment, or a day, or a month, connection is restored. But then the birthing happens, shaped by this cold man-made world. The cutting of the cord is sudden and traumatic, and I am on my own once more. I have to find my way back to Her. Like a baby on its instincts crawling up blindly to its mother's breast to reconnect to the golden flow of Her.

But I know that in the beginning I was Her and She was me. There was no separation. The purest most pleasurable flow of inter-being.

This is what I long for.

This is what I return to. Again and again.

Yet the world has come between us. It did not help me to know Her. To know me. To find this flow. Instead, it silenced Her, hid Her, shamed Her. Silenced me, shamed me... and so I hid.

Often I feel lost in forgetting who She is. Is She just in my imagination? A fanciful notion? Wishful thinking? A desire to replace the god of my childhood with someone who looks more like me? To replace my human mother with an icon? Who is She?

I hold a little sculpture of Her in my hands and I remember Her once more. I could not hold the god of my childhood in my hands. I could not walk on him, curl up against him, immerse myself in him. He was not in my heart, but only looked down at me from on high, judging me. He was forced on me. I could not feel myself in him, sense him pouring through me as I came. Because he did not like sex, my sex, my gender having sex. Instead, I would always be hiding, covering up, shameful of the fullness of my womanly self. Hiding my wildness, in the wildness of the earth and sea and wind and rain, in the labors I was told were my punishment from him for the desire to know.

But in these desires I find Her:

I find Her power and strength, Her tenderness and beauty, Her raw sexuality in the earth and in myself. She is there, integrally. Covered, veiled, hidden, silenced. Waiting. She is there. I touch Her, taste Her, feel Her, see Her and remember myself fully. There is nothing metaphorical about Her. Nothing too much. No shame. No pretense. Sometimes she moves through me like a tiger and sometimes I curl up in the knoll of her grassy belly. And sometimes, when I cannot remember, I hold Her in the palm of my hand and step outside. And as I walk the shoreline and call Her, She is there, more real than I am. She is not a matter of belief. I do not believe in Her any more than I do in myself, if you asked.

I know Her. She is the cycle of the seasons, within and without, the ever-becoming, the creative urge, the pulse of desire, the glow of beauty, the depths of hunger. She is the cave, the cool soil, and the springing shoot. She is solace and destruction, She is honey and the sword. She is the womb of infinite possibility. She is the life in me and the final embrace. She is encoded into every cell of my being.

I am finding the words for what my body has always known.
She is not a matter of belief.
I know Her. I am Her. And She is me.

Hallowed Time
Debra Hall

I bleed and my womb becomes my cave again: the protective sanctuary of my pure potentiality where I can nourish my depths. Here in this darkness is where I can find numinous, interior light. As I rest myself deeply and turn my attention inwards, light streams in through my pineal gland and into my soul. I place one hand on my womb, one hand on my heart and feel into my body, I smile: a quiet, effortless half-smile. As my mind settles, Love comes forward, sometimes bordering on quiet ecstasy. I have experienced this hundreds of times now and after all these years of laboring for presence and peace it has become simple and easy: I no longer struggle and search outside of myself for this union.

One of the most fundamental ways in which I have honored the Goddess—and Goddess within me—over the last twenty plus years has been to make a full silent, solitary retreat, lasting between three and five days, in my home, and other sanctuary spaces, during the bleeding phase of my menstrual cycle. Now that I am on the continuum of Menopause, I make them with the days of the dark moon.

This practice was a norm for our ancestors when women naturally and unquestionably took time to rest and seclude themselves during their bleeding time, not just for their own renewal but also to access the depths of wisdom their transfigured physiology and heightened consciousness enabled, on behalf of their communities. What we are always looking to embrace, I believe, in this ancient Hallowed time is the quality of *depth*, and I hope depth is a word, sufficiently free of associations and connotations that as many women as possible will feel able to include themselves in it. When we touch *depth* within ourselves, we discover how to stay in touch with 'The Self', the *deep* self, Goddess self, the absolute self, presence itself... herself... the life of life... the ground of our being which is Love itself and the wellspring from which every other aspect of our life can blossom and bear fruit.

In this sacred s.l.o.w (shedding the lining of the womb) time I stay close to—feel intimate kinship with nature's simplicity—its 'thereness,' its ability to be itself, so completely. I become more like the things of nature again: a tree's stout trunk, a steadfast rock or stone. I become more like the earth Herself; I notice everything in more detail now that I am as slow and solid and quiet as they are. I crave only my own company I only want myself now... the Self... silence, the boundless spaciousness of pure awareness.

When time and protected space are created, menstrual bleeding allows a depth of healing and renewal throughout all areas and levels of women's physical, emotional and psycho spiritual systems. It is the ideal time for a woman to completely renew and detoxify her body; it is the optimum time to release past traumas and current emotional build ups; it is the time for the soul to reach across the liminal into its rich pool of timeless knowledge, to access expanded states of consciousness, profound inner equanimity and spiritual acuity.

At night I leave my cave and at the same time take it with me. I walk out when there is no one around. I feel drawn to being with outside's different darkness which smells of damp earth and rain. I don't want my face to be seen. Watching, witnessing the world, from behind my face, like some 'other one,' I am detached in a good way and yet am still my most beloved, familiar Self, the one who is looking as if through the eye holes of a mask from this place of true freedom and contentment.

Everything good and productive in my life has come from periodically plugging back into source in this way. Even though my menstrual cycle has always been regular and not unusual or painful, the urge to retreat into solitude and cease all communications with the outside world and other people—even close women friends— has been so overwhelming at every level of my being, that I would have had to actively resist and fight against it, to do anything else.

I love this seclusion, this devotional solitude, this most sacred of interiorities, this cocoon, chrysalis, womb time, moon-blood time, this purring seclusion and 'purda.' Just as nature periodically lies fallow, I am gladly pausing myself and letting go of all that has been and all that I have been in order to surrender completely.

None of us is just one person, we don't have to become caricatures of our selves or choose one identity. Our menstrual cycles allow us to express ourselves and our love in a multitude of ways. When I am premenstrual I feel overwhelming urges towards artistry, activism and creativity. When I am bleeding, I love as a contemplative and a mystic.

When I finish bleeding and enter the follicular phase of my cycle, I want to dance and be energetic, love as a sexual being, joyfully and enthusiastically enact the inspirations and visions that have come through me during bleeding time. When I am ovulating, I want to love the world like a mother, connect with friends old and new, and feel the depths of love that are possible between myself and other people, animals, trees, plants and the Earth herself.

I love knowing that this mystical, embodied Goddess-self dwells in me, that always, when the time is just right, a fresh cycle of growth will be initiated within me, that my hormones—real life angel messengers of wisdom and transformation—will sing me into a new wholeness once again.

The bigger picture of Hallowed Time is that despite the naturally spiritualizing effect that menstruation brings to the whole of a woman's being, ironically it is mainly religions that have demonized menstruation for centuries thus denying us access to this precious gateway. Yet the Goddess urges any of us who have this wisdom to share it, to reach out to girls and women, boys and men—in any way we can—not just for our own sakes but also for the sake of the planet. For it is essential that we re-align ourselves with the ways our bodies intimately mirror the seasonal cycles of nature, in order to stop rampantly consuming and addictively following paths of economic growth that the Earth can no longer bear the burden of, and discover for ourselves that during the times when we outwardly contract—just as nature does in autumn and winter—we inwardly expand making contentment with the simple things of life so much more within our reach.

Goddess Birthing Music

Laura Demelza Bosma

Where I am tired the garden revitalizes me with her soft paws,
welcomes me with her touch on animals' pathways.
Miss Tarantula opening Eden for mammals.

To surround life, the same way life is surrounding me
my steps softly draw the shape of love's pregnant body.
Soon I'm about to turn the inner music inside out.
With lungs gasping, the butterfly will open up fresh wings.
Here, around earth, where longing and air exist to float on.

I imagine this, then turn back to what is:
Rhythms pulsing without my interfering.

The primal woman with cow horn-earrings carrying
water uphill wiggles her hips on stillness's deep beat.

Birthing music is the blood-flower's expression.

Birthing Rites

Ginny Brannan

Instinct guides the body's role
while clock stands still upon the wall
a new moon rises, veiled and hidden.
Contraction peaks, I cede control,
the day expends and evening falls.

Suspended somewhere time has stalled
I see the women I have known
now manifest, emerge before me;
bound in ageless ritual,
joined in sacred unity.

The breath of every life they've sown
emanates from deep within me.
Immersed within this parturition
I realize I'm not alone—
for I can feel their hands upon me.

Increasing in intensity
drawing closer with each wave
I ride the crest before the crown
surrendering all modesty
inside these throes a child is born.

The pain recedes, my newborn cries
and somewhere in me, goddess rises.

Forgive Me

Paraschiva Florescu

Out of her palms birds spurt out,
a pleasing pitying of turtledoves
and when she dances, the threads, thinly etched on the white skin,
paint the air with delicacy
and fate--irregular contours growing towards north, east and
south
and west
and everywhere else.
Her wrists rise up and the blue roads under her skin traverse up
and down
carrying a red life of cells hope oxygen love.
The earth is slightly tilted dragging its hurried souls
down, down. But she is not scared of falling or of darkness.
Her body swirls and drops
like a pen scribbling some inked poetry.
Piano keys white black, an imperfect symmetry,
wield her small and incapable fingers
yet capable of shaping his world and hers—
she is a sculptor of happenings.
The notes expand like balloons and a new story
grows out of the music.
She now knows: nothing will dissolve her scars
and wipe the blood off her feet
but her own hands.
No cursed mouth of a strange man will mend her. There is no need
for compassion.
She offered her narrow neck to the sea,
her eyes to trees, her skin compressed on the paths of mountains,
her arms, legs becoming branches, her mouth becoming leaves,
her blood
rivers.
She swallows her face that echoes on the surface of lakes.
The reflections of a woman entangled in unsought lives,

unchosen paths and lovers,
are gone. She asks for forgiveness.
The black hole that he dredged in her body
deepened each time she loved. She fills the hole with her own
breath.
She invites me in her chimeric dance—me, a broken
body full of cracks and faults. Her hands even my wrinkles
and my pain crumbles between her fingers.
Today, I fell in love so deeply with her.
My heart is bewildered at this indivisible love that only now was
found.
I no longer need you, or anyone else.
Today, I fell in love with myself.

Listen

Anita Grace Brown

Hear the you desiring all the foodstuff, all the yummy drinks?
See her, love her—she's the youngest one inside, still frightened
she'll starve and be no more

Hear the you hoarding all the shiny things, all the green stuff?
See her, love her—she's barely walking now, very unsteady on her
feet

Hear the you shouting WHO AM I???
See her, love her—she's asking the most valid questions of all

Hear the you daring to love the ones who will break her heart?
See her, love her—she's so brave and vulnerable
She's growing up into quite a lady

Hear the you trying out her voice?
speaking truth in love...speaking truth in anger
speaking, writing, shouting, whispering, mumbling
See her, love her—she's not sure you are listening
She's pretty convinced NO ONE is

Hear the you intuiting her life?
Imagining her connecting to God, the rocks crying out, the trees
waving at her, applauding her goodness
See her, love her—she's learning a new language now
deciphering her body's tension, her tears, her goosebumps

Hear the you answering the great call?
Love is guiding her, the river is flowing through her
some days she's sure that she's drowning
others, she's floating and overcome with wonder

gratitude
longing
hope

a prophet for our age
pouring out
for all to join in this kingdom
of heaven coming down

We Are She

Ulli Stanway

There are times when we get deeply hurt. Times, where we stand knee deep in our own muck, no light in sight. Our bodies ache from injustice and manipulation. It seems that no matter how far we have come on our journey, suddenly we are back in the little box of our apparent 'not enoughness.' Even our minds tell us that we are indeed too small.

Yet when we lie wide awake at 2 a.m. She visits. Sometimes quietly, often like a thunderstorm within our minds. She awakens our wisdom and rekindles our wild hearts into their own truth. She does not take 'no' for an answer. Her fierce love for our tender hearts relights our soul's fire.

She wants us to bow to no one. She tells us that we are so much more than enough and that we must break open. Because closing down is no longer an option. She asks us to rise through the darkness and feel all. We must transform our pain into truth and thus heal ourselves. She knows not of fear. She pierces our hearts in search of our courage.

Because. We are enough. And our tender thunder hearts are filled with love and beauty. Even on the darkest of days. Because. We are She. And She is all there is.

So let me gift you with an offering. When my life was drowned in darkness, She visited and asked of me to spill ink onto paper. At 2 a.m. (She does not believe in sleep.)

May these words find their way into your heart and lift your spirits. You are love, beauty and courage. Remember this. Always...

We are the mothers and daughters of this earth
Many have tried to silence us
Many still try to fit us into tiny boxes
We have been called too much and too sensitive
We have been called hysterical
We have been abused, manipulated and treated without heart
Yet, here we are

Rising up with each other
Embracing a new sisterhood
Held gently within Her ancient arms
We decide to speak up and stand for our truth
We allow the feeling of all and we are gentle with our own hearts
No longer are we defending and explaining our own stories
Our cycles are a curse no longer, but a blessing of monthly wisdom
Our bleeding shall no longer be condemned but embraced in its
    sacredness
We now choose freedom and the art of caring for ourselves deeply
    above fitting in
No longer will we make ourselves smaller to please
Our love runs deeply and our wisdom is needed now more than ever

And through all times
She bears witness to her daughters
As we rise one by one
Leaving behind the shackles of patriarchy
For we shall shout our wisdom from the rooftops
We are no longer victims
We are no longer filled with toxicity from a society that embraces
    coldness and logic only
We live life in 6D and full circle of feeling all
We are not static but dynamically flowing in sync with her sacred
    cycles
We are breaking open, wide open and we are without fear
We are free
We Are She
We are We
And by the number of three, so mote it be
She is awaiting our return
And She bows to no one
And neither shall we
We are She
Inspired by Her spirit
So mote it be

The Many Faces of a Goddess

Angel Dionne

A *Goddess Wears Many Faces:*
She wears the face of a mother, sixty-seven years of age, who collects the years in her pockets like smoothed pebbles weighing heavy against the seams. Each pebble an experience, a broken heart, a moment of redemption. She wears the beauty of her scars like a silk scarf. Her eyes, pieces of sea glass the color of spring berries.

She wears the face of a fourteen-year-old niece, soon to be fifteen. A niece standing on the precipice of life, teetering on the brink of adulthood. She yearns for the taste of experience, reaches out her painted fingers to grab life by the stem. She sinks her teeth into life's bitter peel, its sugared flesh and its tough unrelenting pit. The urgency and passion of youth roar past her and she jumps, hoping to find ground. But her feet remain suspended in air for just awhile longer, just awhile longer until they take root.

She wears the face of a wife with nothing but twenty-three years under her belt. She whirls dizzily towards a dream almost realized. Her eyes fixed on books. Her fingers poised on pages of medical jargon. Her hopes firmly planted in the sterile halls of a hospital E.R. Her dedication is sensed by strangers. It drenches her to the tips of her hair, seeps into her skin, and blooms within her belly: a fiery amaranthus.

She wears the face of a friend, three times a mother after losing her own. A friend with wind chime laughter singing gently in the breeze, warbling melodiously during a storm. Her three daughters, three different faces all their own.

She wears the face of a sister, immune to the prying expectations of others. A sister who says 'no' to motherhood, says 'no' to being a wife, says 'yes' to a life lived by her own standards. A sister with a temper the color of pomegranates. She stands with eyes set to the horizon, fists clenched and ready to shatter walls.

My son was born on a snowy December eve. There were moments in labor when I felt like a bystander, watching from out-of-body as some baser instinct carried me through this experience.

I felt overcome with the knowledge that I had become part of something bigger—initiated into the "sisterhood of motherhood." It is probably the singular most spiritual moment of my life.

Illumination

Ginny Brannan

I am mother, daughter, sister, friend
partner, wife, lover, *soulmate...*

I am the sacred feminine.
I have carried new life in my womb
and the weight of the world on my shoulders.
My arms have comforted the crying baby
hugged the wounded child,
held the heartbroken adolescent
caressed the shoulders of my lover
supported the dying parent.
I have defended the weak
cared for the homeless
nursed the sick
I've worked hard and long
that my children will never know hunger,
will *always* have a place to call "home";
and if *'home'* be not shelter but *concept*
then *I* am the embodiment of *that* concept.
I am mentor and spiritual guide
illuminating right from wrong,
compassion from cruelty,
respect from insolence,
intelligence from ignorance.
I am a chronicler of stories
and defender of truth,
ever wise to abstract lies and misdirection.
And in spite of any flaws or imperfections
        I will *still* and *always* be
        —more than you will ever understand
        —more than you could ever imagine:

        I AM the sacred feminine
        —all life is borne through me.

Dancing Goddess

Kim Buskala

I am a dancer
I come from within
all my glory, my peace, my sin

dancing reveals to me
the places I've been
and yet to come

come slowly
birthing seedlings
growing exposing

an open heart, a closed mind
a victory
someone I left behind

lost in the shadow
of yesterdays shine
so bright the dance

as I find a tune
under the moonlight
of a full moon

shadow dance, "I hear the moon say"
make it up
as if it were play

the ins the outs
the dips the falls
roll away, roll away, as if a ball

I do, become the moon
expanding, contracting
as she appears to do

a ball, yes, I must attend
dressed as a princess, all glittered in blue
with glass slippers?

no, barefoot
and pregnant
a messy bun will do

the looks, the stares
I go unnoticed
as I sometimes do

a superpower, we all must possess
when we choose to attend a ball
underdressed

so do they pretend, not to stare
is it pity they feel
do they think I can't be real

real I am, beyond their knowing
dancing, glowing
fading slowing

dreaming
of the day to come
where everyone is engaged in fun.

Goddess Reawakening The Earth
Durdica Mederic

For some decades, a mysterious presence has been communicating with me. Sometimes I have heard its subtle message through spiritual revelations, dreams and channelings, at other times it has been a serendipitous encounter on the Internet or the re-examination of a simple jotting in my notebook.

Its voice guided me: opening up new pathways in my heart, body and mind, and making them work together as a whole. It had allowed me to harness vital energies within, and helped me give birth to new creative adventures, including the book I am currently writing.

Early one morning three years ago, as I lay half awake in bed, I heard the same familiar voice. I had been struggling with chronic illness, or, as I had come to see it, journeying through the underworld, for seven long years. It had been difficult to make sense of my illness, and the day before I had asked the universe for guidance. What was the purpose of my illness? What was I meant to learn?

The voice I heard that morning was crystal clear and filled with intentionality. 'Your illness is part of a divine plan, and has been sent to slow you down,' the voice began. 'It is allowing you to take a step back, to create a space for reflection and to birth new ways of being, ways that are in alignment with your true nature and which will allow you to embody your feminine power. You are invited to bring forth the real power of the divine feminine into your body.'

Instantly things made sense. Although I had heard similar messages before, I had not always been able to fully understand, or I had resisted, or the time hadn't been right for me to receive the wisdom within. My mind simply hadn't been able to see these signs for what they were.

A gentle new energy started to course through me, unmistakable and irresistible, and I knew that I was being given exactly what I needed to persevere on my soul's path, dark and overgrown as it then was.

To my astonishment, I was able to see my illness in a new light. It was a benevolent force that had created my illness, not to serve as mere physical dysfunction, but as a catalyst for relating to myself and to my body in deep ways that I had never previously considered. I found that I was being led by an invisible, compassionate hand to behold, appreciate and love the sacredness of my body in its entirety, even those parts that had been cursed by means of old patriarchal control—the female body been criticized, trivialized, exiled or obscured. Sadly such values have remained in our society today as we have rendered them our own.

My illness was to be the turning point in reinstating my birthright, an expression of authentic divine feminine power inherent within my body's consciousness. I found myself being guided towards a long-forgotten knowledge that regarded the world in very different ways. From a heap of broken fragments, I was given the chance to reassemble a beautiful mosaic. It allowed healing to arise out of my body's innate wisdom, and its subtle message would always guide me home.

I knew that it was my fate to walk with my guide, and with her by my side I was ready to enter any crucible. The fire would consume the remnants of my wounded self, my feelings of unworthiness, of being tamed or shamed, and I would arise from their ashes, a firebird free and graceful and present.

I look upon my connections with the significant people in my life, spiritual catalysts who have inspired me towards deeper learning and soul growth. I look especially upon the women in my life, not just friends and relatives, but also those with whom I may have crossed paths just once. Our encounters were not, it seems, just chance meetings, but intrinsically woven into my soul's plan, creating a tapestry of intimate, loving and mutually sharing bonds.

And so here I am, my heart full of gratitude for the endless blessings I have and will continue to receive. I am grateful for this vital nurturing presence that has appeared on my path of reawakening feminine mystery, for the inner compass that always shows me the gifts of within, that knows how to navigate through dark terrains, how to persevere and accept what is often hard to accept. I acknowledge this ever-present devotional companion and her undying protection. I bow deeper to this initiator of the highest order—witch, shamaness, priestess, goddess, mother.

I am her many faces. We are echoes of each other. We come home together with the shared yearnings for a life that is fuller, wilder and deeper.

Goddess of the Divine Within Us

Nancy Carlson

Coming into my-self
Feeling my own energy
Touching my own essence,
Ever so lightly.
Bringing all of the parts
Of one's self, into harmony
Remembering who I really am.
Being in the moment
That always is, only is.
Connection to self
Connection to others
Connection to earth
Connection to sacred
Whole...wholeness
Being beauty
Being light
Being love
Connection to the Divine within...

Aren't We All

Kim Buskala

The Goddess is Me
I was told at birth
your light will shine
bright for all the world to see

The Goddess is She
the one that births
the beauty we see
the light that shines
so bright

The Goddess of Light
the one so bright
yet blinded by the light
one cannot see
the beauty is she

The Goddess of Darkness
comes without light
searching for soul
digging, digging, deeper, deeper
for what will she see

The Goddess of hope
dreams yet unseen
imagination
the gleam
of a single spark, a single seed

The Goddess of Growth
she under the soil, rooted
in search of the light
fighting to break ground
She believes

Off the Deep End

Shannon Crossman

Only in the arms
of the Beloved
am I free to
let go.
I tiptoe up to
the edge of
myself
and dive off.
She is always
there like some
Divine net
strung across
the chasm
waiting to
catch me as
I fall.
Now, I excel at
falling. Off
rooftops, cliffs,
edges of my mind.
I soar over
the ends
perfecting my
tuck and roll,
sticking the
landing straight
into Her arms
every time.
Come with me
some time.
Feel for yourself
the glorious
nature
of being
eternally
caught.

She

Kimberly DuBoise

She lives in me,
has a dream for me,
watches to see what I will do
with her gift;
she lives through me,
embraces me,
waits for me
to embrace her.
We are inseparable,
this love and I.
We are one.

Feminine Ties, Spirit Wise, Fireflies Souls Rise

Michelle Caporale

I am a woman of love sent from above to do nothing but love. Placing all of your agendas aside, I ride the waves of the oceanic tide. I swim in the depths of the Ionian Mediterranean waters wide. I splash in the seas where only love can abide.

See, I am a lady of love sent from above to do nothing but love.

Placing all of your comments away I hear the jubilation of God's way. I dance the insults astray along with the compliments at bay. I watch for the deep listening wind's sway and blow into the glass bowl of the smoking fire's ashtray. I inhale the peace of Yahweh in the river of love's stay in the current of the Holy One's Bay under the north star-guided ancestral highway, in love's arms I restfully lay.

See, I am a girl of love sent from above to do nothing but love.

Placing all of the injustices that appear out of the engine's gear where visibility is clear, I let His Holiness steer and all the control I thought I needed disappears. Love appears and reappears; peace honking horns I hear; stop signs adhere; commandments beware; no bumper sticker needed to declare faith's unlabeled gears, the joy encircling wheel wares, the love journey clears, the fog of hate disappears and it carries away all of the fears carried as cargo for years, shifting gears.

I am love. She is love. We are divinely united feminine love. Sent from above to do nothing but love. Connecting us all. Joining trinity's call. Elevating energy, peaceful synergy, feminine divinity, uniting as one shining sun flame in the bonfire-risen one. We are all one love. Female soaring creation from above; impregnating animals of Earth, feeding the fetal rebirth; delivering our God-appointed worth. A child born out of the harvested corn in fields of fiery scorn warded off maloik horn, lighthouse forlorn. A gift of hope bundled, ribboned grace to adorn.

The presence of salvation reborn!

The presence of salvation reborn!

A Woman Wilding

Lana Maree Haas

old and stale
breathing shale
sloughing off
heartbeat tales.

dancing on the grieving floor.

find a rhythm,
find a step.
regale the drumming sounds
and let them fall
a steady sprawl
loosened down
upon the shaking ground!

there is more!
there is more!

dancing on the grieving floor.

she can feel me
she's my sanctuary.
when all of my anger
from my steady hallow grief
becomes a crying naked noise.
breathing in the stabbing past,
spewing out the acrid ash.

shall I be all that?
where's the room for
a woman gone mad?

there is more!
there is more!
dancing on the grieving floor.
raging in a dance,

shaking in a trance!
a pining, pitching fervor,
a rumbling, messy murmur.

where do I stand
when I've lost my place?
my true north has no stay!

there is more!
there is more!
dancing on the grieving floor.

I flail and I flaunt
without a thought,
and she accepts
(and celebrates!)
movements big or small.
smooth or jerky,
sensual or smart,
spent or wanting.

there is more!
there is more!
dancing on the grieving floor.

I am bleeding tears into her ample chest,
I am melting skin
and diamond sweat.
I am reborn on
wooden floors!

I am turning into flowing flood waters,
fists and fingers claw the shattered altar,
dancing like a woman wilding!

shall I be all that?
where's the room for
a woman gone mad?

there is more!
there is more!
dancing on the grieving floor.

The Warrior Goddess
Ilda Dashi

She has the courage to dive within her own ocean
and meet her own windy storms
while they make love to her tide's ebbs and flows.

She dares to look deep within
not wanting to escape her demons
as they sail in her empty boat of memories.

She does not run away
when she sees her wild wolves
dance between her past and present life,
at that fine shore of her imagination.

She writes a new story every day
for every moment contains death
and rebirth to her.

She gets along well with her vulnerability,
building a home inside of her fragility.
For she knows strength and weakness
are two sides of one coin,
always co-existing.

She has learned the art of
riding her fear...
unafraid of showing her wounds any longer.
For she knows she will be broken
dissatisfied,
disappointed,
or mad.
As other times she will be blissful:
embracing the full range of human emotions
and creating magic out of them!

She knows that to be a goddess
she also needs to be a peaceful warrior
as both masculine and feminine live within her:
sustain her beautiful being.
Her mind is horizons out of reach
as stars are born in her sky every night,
and her heart is made of a profound intelligence
rising upon each horizon with every heartbeat...
like a compass showing her the next step on the road.

She knows she can get complicated at times
because she feels life so deeply,
thinks too widely
dreams big.

She knows that hurt relates to feeling life deeply.
She allows life's growing pains to take a seat inside her heart.
She knows that making mistakes is human
and that she learns from them what she can't in any other way.

She sees both the beauty and the beast within herself:
as the soft and the wild dance a tango of a million steps inside of her.

She knows that she is beautiful
when she looks into her own eyes in the mirror
knowing her insecurities are like messy rooms
she still needs to clean up.

She knows the power of her tears
to bring her closer to herself.
After all this, she feels her being composed of stars,
and dressed with moonlight,
as she is...
the warrior goddess!

Devotions

Julia W. Prentice

If I am beloved of Goddesses
I will speak my devotions
Out loud, to their ken
Beseeching their ear

Hope against all
That they will be listening
Waiting my praise
From open, grateful lips

I want to bathe in the
Infinite galaxy of divine love
To splash in starlight
Raining down from

Some otherworldly
Place of heaven or
Salvation promised
Given freely

Offered like golden fruit
Plucked from ether
And passed down
To begging hand

Then I will sing
Devotion to their
Oceans of
Universal Love

About the Authors

MANDY ADAMS works as a Menstruality Educator offering Women's Workshops, Online Mentoring, Rites of Passage Ceremonies, and Pregnancy and Well Woman Yoga classes. She is also founder of Red Tent Cornwall and is an online mentor at Red School committed to supporting women awakening to their menstrual journey. www.mandyadams.co.uk

IRMA AGUILAR-OLIVAS: Beginning from a tender age to present day, writing has been a source of immense growth and healing for Irma, providing a window for introspection upon where she weaves her way through the labyrinth of her soul. She is a published first-time author, a wife, mother, and grandmother.

VRINDA AGUILERA is a second-generation practitioner of Bhakti yoga, writer, and poet. She has been joyfully engaged for many years as a Montessori early learning teacher-guide at the Bhaktivedanta Academy in Alachua, FL. She is inspired by the wonder and beauty of nature, engaging in and supporting others in all kinds of creative expression, growth and healing. Her poetry has been published in the "Journey of The Heart" anthologies, *Bhakti Blossoms: A Collection of Contemporary Vaishnavi Poetry* anthology as well as being featured on online publications Rebelle Society and River of Milk e-zine. You can connect with her at vrinda.aguilera@gmail.com.

RHEA RUTH AITKEN walks her spiritual path in Cornwall UK as a Creatress, Communicator of Spirits, Daughter of the Goddess and Writer of Poetry, Stories and Songs. Passionate about the rising feminine, this wonderful earth, good books, art, coffee, the moon and magic she can be found at www.rhearuthaitken.co.uk.

SANDRA M. ALLAGAPEN comes from Mauritius where most of her family still lives. She considers herself truly blessed to have come from a lineage of strong, kind and loving women and men, who have given her the courage to listen to the call of her spirit and move to England. Since then, she has achieved more dreams than she ever thought possible, but her family is still what she is most proud of. She dreams of spending more time in Italy one day and loves books, crystals and autumn evenings.

CHERYL ANNE BRATMAN enjoys a simple life of prayer and presence; open to, and ever seeking, what is Honest and Beautiful. She is mother to three exquisite beings, and friend to many more. Her deepest joy is found in encountering Divinity along the way; in the certainties and surprises of each ordinary day. She believes strongly in the power of warm smiles, gentle breezes, and happy songs.

CHAMELI ARDAGH is a passionate practitioner of embodied feminine spirituality, the founder of The Awakening Women Institute and the Yogini Ashram retreats in Greece and India. She also facilitates leadership trainings and online Shakti Sadhanas, and she is especially appreciated for her passionate love of mythology and storytelling as a method for spiritual awakening and embodiment. She is the initiator of an international network of Women's Temple Groups, and the author of two books on feminine spirituality and embodiment. www.AwakeningWomen.com

CHELSEA ARRINGTON is a second-degree priestess in Twilight Spiral Coven. She loves to compose sacred poetry for ritual and to raise-up her voice in song to honor The Goddess. She lives in the Inland Empire with her Viking Lars, her nephew John, and two papillons Mimi and Chloë.

HAYLEY ARRINGTON has an M.A. in women's spirituality. Her writings have been included in SageWoman, Eternal Haunted Summer, and elsewhere. She is a priestess of Hera and a member of Twilight Spiral Coven. Born and raised in the Los Angeles area, she still lives there with her husband and son.

FATEME BANISHOEIB is a strategic leadership consultant for teams and organizations seeking transformational change. She is the founder of ReNEWBusiness a think tank and consulting firm that helps leaders architect their organizations for innovation, inclusivity and integrity. A published poet, her latest book *The Whisper,* charts the journey from leadership of self to leadership of others.

NANCI BERN is a healer, writer, eco-art therapist, spiritual leader, teacher and coach. She is ever in awe of the spectrum of life. Her goal is to infuse and inspire her clients, students and readers spirits with healing, humor and the thoughtfulness of natural inquiry. Nanci's essays, non-fiction, and poems have been featured in various outlets and recurring columns. Her poems have also been composed to, performed, danced to and displayed. She has also written and performed comedy, theatre and produced. As a healer, social justice worker and trauma professional, she writes articles, creates workshops and wrote a trauma survivor's workbook. www.in-sighthealing.com

SHAVAWN M. BERRY'S work has appeared in *The Urban Howl, Sable Books' Red Sky—On the Global Epidemic of Violence Against Women, Trickster, Huffpo 50, elephant journal, Olentangy Review, Black Fox Literary Magazine, Rebelle Society, The Cancer Poetry Project* 2 and *Poet Lore.* In 1998, she received her MPW in Professional Writing from the University of Southern California in Los Angeles specializing in Creative Nonfiction and Memoir. She teaches writing online for Arizona State University. You can follow her on Facebook and read her work on The Wonderland Files or on her website, shavawnmberry.com. She lives in Santa Fe, NM.

CYNTHIA BLANK received her MFA in Poetry from Bar Ilan University's Shaindy Rudoff Creative Writing Graduate Program. Her work has been featured most recently in Varnish Journal, Escapism Literary Magazine, Anapest, Ithaca Lit, Black Napkin Press, and Lilith Magazine.

LAURA DEMELZA BOSMA (1986) is a mother of three, doula, artist and poetess. She studied and graduated in 'Writing for Performance' at the art-academy in Utrecht (NL). In her poetry book, *The Call Of the Ink Bird,* Laura writes from an outspoken feminine perspective, treating the words the same way she would the organic vegetables that she lovingly cooks meals from. A children's book with a lot of bright pictures about natural childbirth is in the making. www. laurademelzabosma.com

GINNY BRANNAN resides in Massachusetts with her husband, son and three cats. Drawing inspiration from life, nature, and the human condition, her poetry has been published in four previous anthologies. She is honored to be included in this newest collection from Journey of the Heart. Learn more and follow at www. insideoutpoetry.blogspot.com

JHILMIL BRECKENRIDGE is a poet, writer and activist. She is passionate about issues of women, disability, and mental health. Jhilmil is currently working on a PhD in Creative Writing from the University of Central Lancashire in the UK. She is Fiction Editor for South Asian leading literary journal, Open Road Review and is Editor for The Woman Inc. She has recently founded a charity in India, Bhor Foundation and one of their initiatives is to take poetry as therapy into asylums and prisons.

YVONNE BREWER lives in Cork, Ireland and likes to mostly hide her poems and creativity from the world except when she finds a group of soul poets who allow her to burn her poetry flame brightly.

ANITA GRACE BROWN lives in NJ with her husband and golden retriever, Sierra. Their young adult children both attend Syracuse University. They live by the family mantra, "Either everything is a MIRACLE or nothing is!" She enjoys keeping life simple: filling each day with natural beauty, writing, yoga, cooking and meditation. Writing, as spiritual practice and connection has deepened the natural healing and awareness of life's blessings. Anita Grace enjoys sharing her gifts with the physically incarcerated while recognizing many of us are not liberated from the trappings of the mind. You can find her at SmilingheartYoga.org.

KIM BUSKALA considers herself a modern day goddess with Old World influences. She appreciates the ability to travel to faraway places, seeking sites that remind her of how life used to be. The simple pleasure of dancing fills her heart with happiness. Nature, she loves to explore. The bounty, the beauty and the richness only nature can provide. Kim strives to be a reflection of that which Mother Earth supplies. She feeds her soul in love.

MICELLINA CAPORALE is a poetess, prophet, and healer whose writing reflects her belief in the goodness of this world and the greatness, which is to come. Her work can be found within the realms of your own creative spirit and in the hands of giggling children. She is inspired by the spontaneity and courage that youth bring to new moments and sees herself as a lifelong teacher and student.

NANCY CARLSON I am an evolving poet, writing mostly as reflection, contemplation, gratitude, devotion, and as a way of insight into the 'unknown'. I work as an Ayurvedic Health Consultant, Integrative RN Health/Wellness Coach and teacher, yoga teacher and Reiki Master. You may contact me on Facebook or my website, Joyful healing.

SAMIEL CAROLINA'S work is based on a lifetime of studying the feminine. Her personal journey to fully embrace and embody her Soul took her from exploring body-work techniques, to quantum psychology, alternative therapy, energy healing and spiritual South American traditions. As a deeply intuitive peaceful warrior as well as a speaker, writer and international retreat leader, Samiel's mission is to transform the world into a safe space to express ourselves and love each other. She offers women a way to access their unique gifts to come back to a place of peace, clarity and creativity in moments of deep transformation. www.samielcarolina.com

KAI COGGIN is a former Houston Teacher of the Year turned poet and author living in the valley of a small mountain in Hot Springs National Park, AR. She received her B.A. in English, Poetry, and Creative Writing from Texas A&M University. Her work has been published or is forthcoming in *Sinister Wisdom, Assaracus, Calamus Journal, Lavender Review, Anti-Heroin Chic, Luna Luna, Blue Heron Review, Yellow Chair Review,* and elsewhere. Kai is the author of two full-length collections, *Periscope Heart* (Swimming with Elephants, 2014) and *Wingspan* (Golden Dragonfly Press, 2016), as well as a spoken word album called *SILHOUETTE* (2017). Her poetry has been nominated twice for The Pushcart Prize, as well as Bettering American Poetry 2015, and Best of the Net 2016. www.kaicoggin.com

PRANADA COMTOIS is an advocate of the spiritual evolution of Bhakti's wise-love in our lives, our heart, and our relationships. At sixteen she began her lifelong practice and study of Bhakti under the guidance of her guru A. C. Bhaktivedanta Swami. An activist in women's spiritual empowerment, she successfully organized global steps against gender injustice and published a quarterly journal advocating women's rights in the modern Bhakti tradition. She is a featured speaker in the film "Women of Bhakti" and the author of *Wise-Love: Bhakti and the Search for the Soul of Consciousness* (forthcoming). She blogs at www.pranadacomtois.com.

A.B. COOPER has work published online and in print and works as guest editor for Paper Swans Press. Her novella *Lykke and the Nightbird*—a Swedish fairytale—is due for publication this year. Working on her first novel, a ghost story for adults, she enjoys the dark side. Carpe Noctem.

J. ELLEN COOPER An ecologist by trade J. Ellen Cooper's poetry is a reflection of the world through a lens that picks up on the web between the details. She lives on Sydney Harbor with her children and bunny. Delighting in anarchy, she transcends borders, using imagination to stimulate scientific education, and science to inspire art.

ROBIN R. CORAK has had a life-long love of writing and her work has been featured in publications including *Flower Face* (*Bloduewedd Anthology*), *The Sisterhood of Avalon, 2014 Datebook*, *PWP's 2012 Yule Anthology*, and *The Tor Stone*. You can visit Robin at her website www.peacelovemischief.com.

LINDA M. CRATE is an author, writer, and poet from Pennsylvania. She was born in Pittsburgh but raised in the rural town of

Conneautville. Her works have appeared in numerous anthologies and magazines both online and in print. She has four published chapbooks the latest of which is *My Wings Were Made To Fly* through Flutter Press (September 2017). She is also the author of the Magic Series published by Ravenswood Publishing and their imprint Chimera. The latest of these books published was "Corvids & Magic" (March 2017).

MARE CROMWELL As a Medicine Woman/Lightworker/Healer, Mare Cromwell has devoted her life to the Great Mother and midwifing the New World. Her award-winning books include *The Great Mother Bible.* Mare has been told that her work with Mother Gaia is in the prophecies. She is the Visionary behind the 1000 Goddesses Gathering. www.marecromwell.com

SHANNON CROSSMAN is a wanderer, poet, and long-time seeker who at last exhausted her will to look outward for answers. These days she is much more interested in the art of examining what can already be found within. She is a creative tsunami, rabid devourer of books, meditator, technical wizardress, public speaker, Goddess worshipping priestess, gluten-free baker, time-bender, and COO who happens to possess a degree in Transpersonal Psychology. She's also a mama and a grandma to a gaggle of wild girls who make her heart happy. Shannon still believes in magic, craves the ocean like a land-locked mermaid, and dreams of a life without shoes.

ALYSCIA CUNNIGHAM is an entrepreneur, author, filmmaker, photographer, wife, mother of three children and a creative soul. Her previously published book, *Feminine Transitions,* and upcoming documentary film and coffee table book, 'I Am More Than My Hair,' are social-change projects that challenge society's beauty standards. Alyscia started journaling as well as writing poems and short stories at the age of ten, and has kept it all in her memory box. She says one day she'll have the pleasure to sit with her children and read to them some of her childhood writing. Connect with her on Facebook or visit her website.

ILDA DASHI is a former journalist/reporter, freelance writer, poet, free-thinker, freedom lover and author of *It is You Searching For You*, (February 2017). Having graduated in journalism with a Masters degree, and holding a bachelor degree in psychology, she has a rich experience of ten years of expertise in the field of broadcasting media (TV and radio) covering mostly the economical, political and social issues in her country of Albania. After much reflection, Ilda left these two careers to dedicate her time and energy to exploring the science of the soul, inner growth, meditation and healing. Find her on Facebook and Youtube.

JACQUELINE DAVIS I am a mother, gardener, energy healer and a joyfully perpetual student and teacher. Poetry and stories were the first places where I began to reclaim my identity as a being born into a far more alive and multivalent world than the one presented in my formal education. Through writing, the Goddess began to speak to me and I learned of my identity as both a child of the Goddess and as the Goddess herself in one of her many perfect forms. What a brave thing for all of us to claim we emanate from that great Source directly! How much more is possible for ourselves and for the world from this stance.

REBECCA DELEO is dedicated to the marriage of female sexuality and spirituality. As Goddess, Reiki Master Teacher, holistic healer and counselor, linguistic mystic, seer, lady liberator, and Queen of Night, she catalyzes transfiguration of the mind, body, and soul. She unravels the mysteries of the feminine and illuminates all that is woman. She is devoted to awakening women and men to their goddesshood/godhood. Connect with Rebecca via email (r.deleo@ymail.com) or Tumblr (themotherofrevelation.tumblr.com).

REV. MAALIKA-SHAY DEVIDASI has dedicated her life to serving the Healing Arts and The Path of The Divine Mother. An initiate of Sufism, Sri Vidya Shaktism and Tantra, Classical Vedanta Yoga, and Inter-Faith Ministries, her devotion to The Goddess is channeled through mystic poetry, sacred dance, and providing Living Goddess Activations.

Angel Dionne is a professor at the University of Moncton and an interdisciplinary PhD student at the University of New Brunswick. Her area of specialty includes surrealism, existentialism, and the absurd. Her work has appeared in various publications including; *Chicken Soup for the Soul* and *The Penman Review*. Angel is the founder of *The Peculiar Mormyrid Surrealist Journal*.

Theresa C. Dintino is an ancestral Strega (Italian wise-woman), Earth worker, and initiated diviner. Theresa is the author of seven books, including three novels, *The Strega and the Dreamer, Ode to Minoa* and *Stories they Told Me*; as well as *Welcoming Lilith* and a *Tree Medicine Trilogy*. www.ritualgoddess.com

Amanda Dobby is an artist and amateur photographer, a writer, poet and mom. She loves adventuring and dancing with her two beautiful children, exploring and contemplating Mother Nature in all her seasons and glory, getting lost in philosophical books, and passionately scribbling words onto pages in between all the magical madness that is life.

Kimberly DuBoise is a writer and reader of inspiration. She uses poetry as her medium of artistic choice. Drawing from life experiences, she aims to encourage and uplift others through words. She has several poetry books available on Amazon and on her website: www.kimberlyduboise.com

Susan Laura Earhart describes herself as a perpetual student who defines her expression of person by many names: Witch, Tantrika, Devotee of Dark Mother Kali, Lover of Nature and Worshiper of Words, to name a few. Recently, she has discovered the sheer joy in expressing her contemplations and experiences through poetry and prose. Her heart's passion is teaching, which began many years ago tutoring nursing students, and evolved, as she did, into teaching the art of witchcraft and sharing the jewels of ancient Tantra, to help women find their power, their peace and their voice. You can connect with her on Facebook @ Witches of Ahimsa.

GERRY ELLEN is a freelance writer, storyteller, wellness advocate, nature explorer and avid animal lover. She contributes to several online publications and has authored and published two books, *Ripple Effects* (March 2012) and *A Big Piece of Driftwood* (April 2014), both available on Amazon.com. Musings on her and Scout's (her four-pawed companion) adventures can be found at www. eightpawswellness.squarespace.com.

PEGI EYERS is the author of the award-winning book *Ancient Spirit Rising: Reclaiming Your Roots & Restoring Earth Community*, a survey on social justice, nature spirituality, the recovery of ancestral wisdom, and the holistic principles of sustainable living. She is a member of the Helena Clan (world clans descended from "Mitochondrial Eve" as traced by The Seven Daughters of Eve), with more recent roots connecting her to the mythic arts and pagan traditions of England and Scotland. She lives in the countryside on the outskirts of Peterborough, Canada on a hilltop with views reaching for miles in all directions. www.stonecirclepress.com

PARASCHIVA FLORESCU is a Bhakti-yoga practitioner, lover of poetry, martial arts, books and rivers, and—of course—the truth. As a Law student at Edinburgh University she organizes Kirtans and Bhakti Yoga sessions for the student community. Paraschiva is also founder of the Krishna Conscious Society, after having graduated from a Kirtan course in Belgium. Find more of her poems on her blog, where she publishes regularly. Paraschiva can be reached at para.skevi@yahoo.com.

JAZZALINA GARCIA is fond of writing poetry, which—with the help of a filmmaker—she has turned into short films, one of which was a finalist in a film festival. Jazzalina also enjoys expressing through her words the insights that come through her from source as she journeys inwardly "Home" back to wholeness.

GLORIA D. GONSALVES, also fondly known as Auntie Glo, is an award-winning author and multi-published poet. Not just a writer, Gloria is a creative promoter for writing itself: she founded WoChiPoDa.com, an initiative aimed at instilling the love of poetry in young people. Her literary works aim to support humanitarian projects, inspire creativity and moral lessons. When taking a break from writing, she learns how to take lines for a walk. You can find her online at www.gloria-gonsalves.com.

DEBRA HALL I am a soulmaker, dancer, natural healer, rites of passage and mindfulness teacher living in South West Scotland. I am in the process of creating *Hallowed Time*, which is a book of nourishing images, words and 'ways in' for women to access their own depths during menstrual bleeding. It will also be an online platform for women around the world to share their sacred menstruation practices, including a series YouTube videos and articles to proactively reach out to mainstream audiences about the vital relationship between the seasonal cycles of the Earth and women's own: honoring these is a form of eco activism. I am very happy to be contacted at debra.ha@hotmail.co.uk.

AISLEN HARTWELL is a lifelong Pagan who grew up with Magick, Astrology, Shamanism, Divination, and healing. Surviving and thriving after a diagnosis of Complex PTSD, Aislen champions the return of Goddess consciousness, believing that She can help us restore balance and harmony with masculine and feminine aspects of consciousness. Blessed Be.

LANA MAREE HAAS is a poet and a songwriter. She has produced two albums of songs, "Stardust and Moonbeams" and "Riotous Singing!" and contributed to online blogs such as Journey of the Heart and Rebelle Society. She is currently working on her first book of poetry, and her next album.

AMY LEONA HAVIN is a poetess, yogi, dancer spiritual student, wild-woman, and natural beam of light based in Portland, Oregon. An Aquarian, she spends her days penning letters to friends and basking in the summer sun. Her writing began as an exercise in patience and the practice of being heard, and grew to become a career in literature, language, and the arts. She is a constant traveler and true lover of nature, wandering through deserts, hitchhiking the highways, and finding solace in all bodies of water. She is the Artistic Director of Portland-based dance company The Holding Project and has recently released an illustrated book of poems titled *SHAKTI.* Her work can be found at www.amyleonahavin.com.

AUDREY HANEY is a poet and self-taught artist living in Sussex, U.K whose work has been published in books and magazines, both paper and online, in blogs and websites. Many such publications have also contained her art and illustrations. Audrey owns a number of cats, a mad dog and some feathered creatures. You may read more of her poetry on her blog "Audrey Haney's Poetry Page" or connect with her on Facebook.

JANAVI HELD started writing poetry and wandering around with her father's camera as a child. At the age of nineteen, she began practicing Bhakti yoga. She holds a bachelor's degree from Goddard College where she studied poetry, photography, and media studies. She is author of *Letters to my Oldest Friend: A Book of Poetry and Photography,* (August, 2017).

EMELINA HOLLAND (Moon Jaguar Sees the Dawn) I am a High Priestess of Love & Womb Keeper of Sacred Creative Manifestation. A Practical Mystic, Healer, Metaphysical Artist, Author, Educator, Singer, Mother, Sister & Wife. I am also the Founder of the Sacred Flame Sisterhood Circle, Sacred Root Dance, Creative Spirituality, The Creative Womb's Magic & Creative Motherhood Teachings.

JASMINE KANG is a writer from California, who also enjoys art, listening to music and being in nature. Her creative work has appeared in various projects. She is also the author of *River of Light,* an award-winning collection of prose, poetry and artwork. To find out more about Jasmine, visit Moonshinegarden.com.

MAUREEN LANCASTER is a spiritual woman who is continually inspired by the poetry and lessons that she sees within everyday occurrences. Not considering herself a formal writer or poet, she started writing as an outlet for healing and finding wholeness following widowhood with her first book, *Revelations of a Singing Bowl.*

Tiffany Lazic (BAA, RIHR, RP) is a Registered Psychotherapist and Spiritual Director with a private practice in individual, couples and group therapy in Kitchener (Canada) and internationally via Skype. As the owner of *The Hive and Grove Centre for Holistic Wellness*, she created and teaches two self-development programs and has conducted workshops for many conferences and organizations in Canada, the US, Mexico, and the UK. She is the author of *The Great Work: Self-Knowledge and Healing Through the Wheel of the Year* (Llewellyn Publications, 2015). Visit Tiffany at www.hiveandgrove.ca.

Lauren Love currently works as a Montessori Teacher and is passionate about providing a joyful and loving holistic education for the children. She is currently writing a series of magical books for the little ones to inspire, empower and keep their magical spark very much alive. Lauren is also a qualified hypnotherapist and energy healer and is particularly drawn to working with women, including heart and womb healing. She's a lover of heart-full conversation, deep soul connections, nature, creativity, wellness and adventure. You may connect with Lauren via her website laurenlove.co.uk.

Rachel Lyon As a Spiritualist in her thirties I write poetry on the theme of Gaia and Womanhood engaging a sense of finding a natural rhythm in the Earth's core lost under layers of time. I have a deep desire to get back to the connection with life and its beauty. I write poetry to capture this.

Durdica Maderic (UK) Becoming worn out by life, she received a call in 2008. It guided her into depths of her underworld from which she returned few years ago. She recognized it as the journey of reclaiming her authentic feminine power and true voice, which she longs to share in her book. She is blessed with her family and beauty of Surrey Hills. Email glowingviolet6@gmail.com; Facebook titled *She, Moon and Muse* showcases her latest creative adventure.

ANU MAHADEV is a left brained software engineer—turned right brained creative poet! Originally from India, she is now based out of New Jersey, with her husband and son. She is a recent MFA graduate of Drew University and a prolific writer. Other words to describe her are dreamer, choir singer, social bee, book and movie addict, avid hiker, lifelong learner and traveler. She writes mostly about love, life and the ties that bind us. She currently serves as Editor in Chief for Jaggery Lit, as Editor for the Woman Inc. and co-editor for QuillsEdge Press.

DOLLY MAHTANI is a Professional Dreamer, Child of the Universe, teacher of the Raja Yoga practice at Brahma Kumaris University. A writer. A blogger. A poet. An aspiring novelist and screenwriter. A lover. A giver. An optimist, a rebel, a romantic. A breaker of paradigms and stereotypes. A spiritual social worker and activist. Her purpose and passion is to elevate human consciousness; to help people remember who they really are.

TAYA MALAKIAN is a Poet, Artist, Yogini and Mystic. She holds a degree in Religious Studies with a focus on Mystical Traditions. Her lifelong journey has been to go deep into the layers of reality through ritual, journeying, meditation and reflection. Her work is to share the paths to deep wisdom and the ways of bringing soulfulness into every aspect of daily life. She does this by teaching yoga and meditation and through her poetry and artwork.

ZOE MAYNARD is an English BA (Hons) graduate from the UK. Her poetry has featured in *The Poeteer: A 21st Century Poetry Publication*, *Midnight Circus* literary magazine, *Les Rêves des Notre Ours* and in the *Indiana Voice Journal*. Her work has also featured in *The Anthologia, Cauldron Anthology, Vox Poetica, The Wells Street Journal* and in *Aurora: EKU's Literary and Arts Journal*.

CHANDRIKA McLAUGHLIN writes devotional poetry by the inspiration of her beloved Guru Srila Nayayana Maharaja who has returned to the spiritual world to be with Radha and Krishna in Manjari form. She is a Maui based licensed MFT therapist specializing in anxiety and trauma recovery with EMDR and hypnotherapy.

JOAN MCNERNEY'S poetry is in numerous literary magazines including Seven Circle Press, Dinner with the Muse, Moonlight Dreamers of Yellow Haze, Blueline, and Halcyon Days. Three Bright Hills Press Anthologies, several Poppy Road Review Journals, and Kind of A Hurricane Press Publications accepted her work. She has four Best of the Net nominations.

MAUREEN KWIAT MESHENBERG is the author of *Seasons of the Soul: Transitions and Shifts of Life* and a prolific poetess. She is guided by her inner soul's journey and her empathic musings about life. Maureen draws from her human experiences, touching many with her words. She has been published in several poetry anthologies and currently runs "Heart's Calling" her own Facebook page where she reaches over 4,000 readers. Maureen hosts monthly, sacred creative writing circles for women and recites poetry at many local events. She has three adult children and currently lives in Oak Park, Illinois.

ZOE MICHAEL is a passionate Reiki Healer practicing since 2015. Additionally she offers Intuitive Energy Massage, Sound Healing and Soul Journey card readings. Zoe has a wide array of skills with experience and professional work within Retail Management, Theatre In Education, Acting, Student Workshop Facilitating and Teaching. As a passionate people-worker and lover of all things creative, Zoe supports others through their Spiritual awakening. She is currently in the process of writing a book through which she aims to empower the lives of others by teaching self-acceptance, forgiveness and self-love. As Zoe continues her poetic journey she inspires others on their path of self-discovery and enlightenment.

JENNIFER R. MILLER is an inspirational writer, eclectic witch, tarot reader, and priestess. Her passion is exploring and celebrating the Divine Feminine through creative arts, shamanic ritual, and intuitive readings. Her works have been published in *SageWoman* and *Wild Woman Rising*. Follow her at quillofthegoddess.com.

SHAWNDRA MILLER is a writer and energy worker in Indianapolis. A certified ThetaHealing(R) practitioner, she opens her readers and clients to a wider sense of the possible by connecting them with their inherent spaciousness. Connect with her at shawndramiller. com or shawndra@shawndramiller.com.

RESHMA MIRCHANDANI is a business feminist student by day and a writer by night. Topics are autobiographical and emanate from the process of healing from sexual trauma. Her work is described as stream of consciousness *avant-garde* with an easy to relate to sensibility.

ANITA NEILSON is an author, spiritual poet and kindness blogger. Her writings centre around finding the Divine in the natural world, and the joys of devotional meditation and service to others. Initially inspired by a period of life-changing ill-health (she has Fibromyalgia and M.E. (chronic fatigue syndrome), Anita aims to teach others that despite any limitations they have, they *can* make a meaningful contribution to the world around them, by reconnecting with their inner kindness and compassion. She is the author of *Acts of Kindness from Your Armchair* (Ayni Books 2017). Connect with Anita on her blog '*Healing Words: Inspirational Bytes of Calm,*' Facebook or Instagram.

LUCY H. PEARCE is a multiple Amazon bestselling author, vibrant artist, teacher, mother of three and the founder of Womancraft Publishing. www.womancraftpublishing.com. Her most recent book is *Full Circle Health: integrated health charting for women.* Her others include *Burning Woman, Moon Time, The Rainbow Way.* Visit her at www.lucyhpearce.com.

SONJA PHILLIPS is a rising poetess, a free spirit, dreamer and spiritualist. She was born in Chicago and now resides in Texas with her husband and three beautiful daughters. Sonja holds a B.A. in Spanish though her life's passion is poetry. Sonja is author of the books *Living Poetry: Perceptions of a Goddess* and *Erotic Papyrus.* Several of her poems have been published in two forthcoming anthologies. She has an unusual style of poetry, mystical, passionate, otherworldly. Her words are divinely inspired. She hopes to inspire women all around the globe to awaken to the inner goddess.

JACLYN PIUDIK authored two chapbooks, *Of Gazelles Unheard* (Beautiful Outlaw, 2013) and *The Tao of Loathliness* (fooliar press, 2005/8). Her poems have appeared in numerous anthologies and journals, including *New American Writing* and *Columbia Poetry Review*. She holds an M.A. in Creative Writing and a Ph.D. in Medieval Studies.

JULIA W. PRENTICE A deeply feeling Cancer, Julia lives in CA with her soulmate and current furry companion. A former ASL interpreter, current passionate peer supporter of persons with mental health challenges and knitter, crafter and singer. Always driven to write, she writes like breathing: in ragged gasps, deep inhalations, half-voiced whispers.

GRACE GABRIEL PUSKAS fully believes in the power of words and intention to heal and create. She has great respect for all of life and believes it is our humanity which connects us all. A variety of her writings and spoken word poetry can be seen at www. gracegabriella33.wixsite.com/grace. Love is her way.

THEA PROTHERO follows a Druid path and devotee of the Goddess Brigid. She lives in the south of the UK and loves taking photos and tending her allotment trying to be as self-sufficient as possible. Please view her photos at www.theaprothero.co.uk.

CAROLYN (RIKER) AVALANI, MA, LMHC, is a poet and author of *Blue Clouds*. She's a Licensed Mental Health Counselor, teacher and writing coach. She co-edited an anthology with BethAnn Kapansky Wright, called *Hidden Lights* (Sep. 2017.) For more information, please check out her website: www.carolynriker.com.

FRANCES ROBERTS-REILLY is a poet, author and filmmaker. She has a Welsh Romany ancestry. She began writing seriously in 1972, whilst working at BBC television in London, England. After making award-winning documentaries, she earned an Honors degree in English Literature at the University of Toronto. In her Crone years, Frances's Goddess poetry is in Glastonbury Festival's Goddess Pages, ARAS and the Journal of Eco Psychology. Her poem

"Hecate's Suppers" was featured in staging of "Living Goddess Exhibition" in Gulfport, Florida. She performs her family's Gypsy stories with her harp as storyteller.

KRISHNA ROSE is a singer/songwriter, artist, healer and writer currently scribing her forthcoming historical novel about the life of Mary Magdalene: *Magdalene Speaks.* Krishna has been a student of the God and Goddess for decades while practicing Bhakti yoga under the guidance of Swami Bhaktivedanta Narayana who initiated her into the ancient teachings of India.

LEAH SOLOMAA has been a professional singer, actor, dancer and musician since the age of nine. In 2009, she fine-tuned her work to encompass her soul journey and heart centre founding GAIA VOICE: singing for the whole body, mind and spirit. Her *Women's Voices, Women's Wisdom* teachings is a one-on-one soul based coaching practice to help women come into their authentic power. Leah performs live across North America for large symphony orchestras, workshops and in forests or cathedrals. Her voice is her direct link to Mother Gaia and healing energy for a more heart centered planet and consciousness rising Universe. She lives in London, Ontario.

CATHERINE L. SCHWEIG is founder of the "Journey of the Heart Poetry Project," an online forum where women's voices are honored through sharing poetry. This book is the fourth in a series of anthologies to emerge from that project. Her relationship with Nature and the Goddess Radha is at the heart of her spiritual journey. As a Bhakti yoga practitioner since the late 80's, Catherine has also published in several yoga magazines over the years. In 2006, she and her spouse, Graham, cofounded "The Secret Yoga Institute." They live in Virginia with their beloved cat, where Catherine enjoys making art, Waldorf-style dolls, crocheting, reading and writing letters to her two adult sons and close friends. You may reach her on Facebook or email her: catherine@secretyoga.com.

BEATE SIGRIDDAUGHTER, www.sigriddaughter.com, is poet laureate of Silver City, New Mexico (Land of Enchantment). Her work has received several Pushcart Prize nominations and poetry awards. In 2018 FutureCycle Press will publish her poetry collection *Xanthippe and Her Friends* and Červená Barva Press will publish her chapbook *Dancing in Santa Fe and Other Poems* in 2019.

TOSHA SILVER is the author of the books *Outrageous Openness: Letting the Divine Take the Lead* and *Change Me Prayers: the Hidden Power of Spiritual Surrender*. She's known for finding fresh, humorous and practical ways to embrace an Inner communion with the Divine and for avoiding clichés and dogma at all costs. She teaches online in the *Living OO Forum* and in workshops around the world. You can find out more at www.toshasilver.com.

MUMTAZ LAYLA SODHA founder of Surya Therapy is an Intuit, holistic psychotherapist, Reiki Master, Oracle and writer. Layla is the spiritual name that was given to Mumtaz. Layla has dedicated her life to awakening and reclaiming the feminine rebalancing of the Sacred Masculine energy. Her work is about empowering men and women to reclaim fragmented parts of themselves.

CAMELLIA STADTS I have lived in Michigan my whole life. I have a BA in English from Marygrove College in Detroit. I love writing poetry, which seems to set me free somehow and I often get what I call nudgings from my Spirit (the Goddess) that gets the words flowing. When I'm not writing I also enjoy knitting and crocheting and spending time with my grandson.

ULLI STANWAY is an ever-evolving Wordsmith. She is a Poetess on a fierce mission to discover the wide-open spaces within her story. Ulli writes about all things that pierce her tender thunder heart. Her soul mantra is: "RIP Pinocchio. Your strings have served you well but now it is time to skip down your own path; barefoot, if you wish."

ALISON STONE is the author of five collections, including *Ordinary Magic, Dangerous Enough,* and *They Sing at Midnight,* which won the 2003 Many Mountains Moving Award. Her poems have appeared in The Paris Review, Poetry, Ploughshares, and many others. She was awarded *Poetry's* Frederick Bock Prize and *New York Quarterly's* Madeline Sadin award. She is a licensed psychotherapist.

TAMMY STONE TAKAHASHI currently lives in Japan. She loves to express her passion and curiosity through photography, journaling and slow stitching. Her poetry and short stories have been widely published and anthologized, and she has authored two poetry books, *Formation: Along the Ganges and Back Again*, and *Little Poems for Big Seasons*.

ALISE VERSELLA is the 27-year-old author of *Five Foot Voice, Onion Heart and A Few Wild Stanzas*. Her work can be found on Rebelle Society and Entropy among others as well as the previous anthologies from Women's Spiritual Poetry. You can visit her website www.aliseversella.com and connect with her through Facebook and Instagram via these handles: alise versella, poet and aliseox.

LOUISE WHOTTON works with the Goddess and the feminine, in both her academic and spiritual work and is currently working on a book entitled *Reclaiming the Crone,* which is based upon one of the talks she offers at Pagan events.

BETHANNE KAPANSKY WRIGHT is working on chasing rainbows, finding joy, and building her mermaid skills on the beautiful island of Kauai. She is an Intuitive, Psychologist, Writer, and Artist. She is the author of several books including *Lamentations of The Sea,* and is currently writing its sequel, *Revelations of The Light.*

From the Artists

What an honor it is to contribute my artwork to this collection of writings that bears witness to, honors, and celebrates the Goddess within each of us, the Goddess Eternal, and the idea of the Mythical Goddess. The drawings sprung from my experience of the Divine Feminine—her never-ending grace, her presence everywhere in nature, her fortitude, and even her playful light. Most of all, I see the Goddess represented through the nurturing compassion and generative creativity so often found in humans. And so, it is to the Goddess within each of you that I humbly offer these artworks as my expression of appreciation.

Jill Cooper

The acrylic painting on the cover is from my series of 'Medicine Women.' These women come to me—to us—transmitting their messages, their wisdom, their knowledge, their experience, their power, their brilliance and their healing vibrations. They accompany us in life as they reveal and awaken what we bear within ourselves. They remind us our connection with the great All and with Mother Earth. I bring them to live by painting instinctively: I follow my intuition, I listen to my heart and I let myself be guided, I let the colors and patterns come to me, I am only the tool. I paint on a copper foil surface because I love its light, which illuminates the women's worthiness of respect, their sacredness and their majesty.

Caroline Manière

Shailie Dubois has a degree in Psychology and practices Intuitive Prayer Healing, a combination of Christianity, Shamanism, and Aromatherapy. Her poetry and artwork has been featured in three Journey of the Heart anthologies. Shailie is the author and illustrator of *Dani*, a children's book and is busy creating her next picture book.

Jill Cooper is an artist and poet living in beautiful Washington State. Her work has appeared in various print and online journals, magazines, books, galleries, and on stage. Her joy is in knowing the Infinite Divine through nature, meditation and creativity. You may follow her work on Instagram @jilllinnette.

Caroline Manière is a French artist who began studying and directing advertising graphics in Paris for ten years, later returning to her true passion: painting from her heart. Her copper canvass creations spring from inspiration she drew from the richness and diversity of the colors and patterns found in Asian costumes. Caroline's outer travels stimulated deep inner journeys that feed her artwork. Her creative process incorporates music, breathing, dreams, karmic astrology, symbolic rituals, Vedic influences, and other exploratory aids. Learn more about her art online: www.carolinemaniere.com.

I am the unfading beauty of times to come.
In me Grace is at work to divinize the soul.
I shall continue to disclose myself to you.
I am the Eternal Feminine.

Pierre Teilhard De Chardin

Index

Radharani (Radha) v, xiv, 134, 135
Rainbow 28, 45, 104, 131, 142
Rosh Chodesh 37
Ruth 38

Sacred xx, xxiii, 1, 4, 6, 17, 36, 38, 41, 46, 48, 49, 50, 53, 78, 92, 93, 123, 126, 161, 165, 174, 175, 183, 187, 188, 191, 197, 200, 206
Saraswati 106, 149
Shabbat 36
Shailaputri 129
Shakti 129, 148, 149, 153
Sheilagh 13
Shekinah 36, 37, 38, 39, 153
Shiva 129, 130
Siddhidatri 130
Sita xiv
Skanda Mata 129
Sky xxi, 8, 25, 28, 30, 32, 48, 60, 64, 90, 100, 116, 131, 150, 151, 167, 182, 214
Sophia 1, 133
Soul 3, 4, 6, 14, 15, 17, 18, 19, 36, 37, 48, 49, 80, 88, 89, 90, 93, 94, 98, 99, 101, 117, 118, 135, 142, 148, 153, 161, 162, 165, 171, 182, 187, 188, 196, 203, 204, 207, 240
Spirit xiii, 15, 17, 19, 36, 37, 38, 39, 46, 51, 67, 87, 88, 90, 91, 94, 101, 106, 107, 108, 117, 118, 122, 142, 161, 171, 197
Spring xiii, 22, 73, 122, 123, 153, 167, 169, 175, 198
Stars xxi, xxiii, 20, 22, 25, 28, 55, 60, 64, 69, 133, 136, 144, 161, 175, 214
St. Brigid 122
Summer xiii, 73, 122, 123, 169, 177
Surya 129

Tara 25, 26, 106
Tikkun Olam 38
Tonantzin xiv
Torah 37
Tree of Life 37
Tulasi Devi xiv

Turtle 91, 93

Uranus 60

Vajrayogini 25
Vayu 129
Vedic 26
Venus 23, 24, 25, 116, 117, 118, 177
Vishnu 129

Water Goddess 14, 15, 16
White Buffalo Woman 25
Wind 20, 28, 30, 32, 38, 48, 49, 88, 90, 101, 125, 133, 142, 145, 154, 157, 161, 163, 185, 198, 210
Winter xiii, 73, 91, 92, 122, 123, 169, 189
Witch xiv, 21, 42, 105, 167, 168, 205
Wolf 32, 69, 213
Woman xx, 33, 37, 43, 47, 61, 69, 76, 81, 86, 87, 88, 103, 111, 112, 125, 130, 141, 142, 143, 146, 147, 150, 157, 158, 159, 181, 188, 189, 190, 192, 210, 211, 212
Womb xiv, xxiii, 6, 8, 12, 17, 33, 37, 42, 60, 82, 98, 165, 185, 187, 188, 200

Yama 129
Yemanja xiv
Yoga xiv
Yoga Maya xiv
Yoni 168
Yuba 25

Zeus 103

Made in the USA
San Bernardino, CA
25 January 2018